1 CORINTHIANS
A Handbook for Christian Men

Loren VanGalder
Spiritual Father Publications

ISBN-10: 0-9982798-6-2
ISBN-13: 978-0-9982798-6-2

Contents

Introduction

The church in Corinth seemed like a first century success story: impressive growth, changed lives, and abundant manifestations of the Holy Spirit. Yet there were serious problems in the charge, and it was up to Paul to address them. He had planted the church and was responsible before God for it as an apostle of Jesus Christ. But they didn't want to accept his authority!

As Paul works through the various issues that confronted the church he provides us with an invaluable handbook on the church and the Christian life. It is a life so radical that it feels foreign to most of us in the 21st century. It is controversial; you will find many teachings that go against what is commonly taught today. Yet more than ever there is a need to return to the vitality and experience of the first century church.

Are you willing to evaluate your life and church in the light of Scripture? This is not a commentary. My hope is that you will read prayerfully and devotionally, but most importantly, intending to put it into practice. You probably won't agree with everything I say. That's fine. No commentary or study Bible is infallible. But try to look at the Scripture with fresh eyes and an open mind. Rather than just dismiss a difficult passage, honestly grapple with it. Open your heart and mind to the Holy Spirit, and listen to the heart of your Father.

Greeting
1 Corinthians 1:1-3

Nobody likes to open a message on Facebook or WhatsApp to find a rebuke or controversy. There will be rebukes and controversies in his letter as he addresses some serious issues, but Paul opens his letter by greeting the church and affirming their strengths.

¹Paul, called to be an apostle of Christ Jesus by the will of God, and our brother Sosthenes.

Who is this Paul?

Along with a brother names Sosthenes, Paul has written this letter. The Corinthians already know him, but he wants to remind them that:

- He was called. He didn't decide to be a Christian or an apostle. God calls us to obedience and repentance. We can choose to answer or resist that call. Have you responded to God's call to accept Jesus Christ?

- God also calls us to a specific task in the church. Jesus sent Paul as an apostle, to establish and oversee churches. Along with the call comes Christ's authority, which Paul exercises in this letter. Are you aware of your calling? Are you operating in it? Are you experiencing God's authority as a result?

- He can write with authority and confidence because he knows his calling was God's will. God has a plan and purpose for history. His will is supreme. The cry of the believer's heart is "Thy kingdom come, thy will be done." This letter, like all Scripture, reveals his will. Do you want to know God's will for your life? Are you in his will?

- Jesus Christ is his Lord and Master. His aim is to glorify Jesus. He is totally submitted to God's will and calling, leading him to write this difficult letter.

- Paul doesn't work alone. He was always accompanied by another apostle or someone whom he was discipling.

Who is this teaching for?

[2] To the church of God in Corinth, to those sanctified in Christ Jesus and called to be his holy people, together with all those everywhere who call on the name of our Lord Jesus Christ—their Lord and ours.

The letter primarily addresses issues in the Corinthian church, but the teaching is for the church universal. We tend to focus on Jesus as our "personal Savior," and he is, but God is preparing a body, a community of disciples. Paul doesn't address the letter to the pastor, or the elders; God works with us as his people, his church. We need to be an integral part of a local expression of that body of believers.

There are many things Paul could say about the church, but here he chooses to focus on two important characteristics:

- They have been sanctified in Christ Jesus. When they accepted Christ and were united to him, they were set apart from the world, purified, and established as a distinct community. If you are in Christ, you have been sanctified. Do you understand what that means? Do you live it out? Or do you think you will look weird if you do?

- They are not just called to individual holiness, but corporately, to be a holy people. God has already set us apart - but we haven't arrived yet. We are not perfect. We have the call and know the goal, but we are still in process. It is part of the tension of living in this world. Unfortunately the Corinthians were not all that holy. Paul will encourage them to greater holiness, to bring their daily experience closer to what God has already done in them.

We find unity with other believers in our common relationship to Jesus as Lord. If he is not in first place in our lives and the church, unity will elude us. There should be a deep bond since we all serve the same Lord.

A blessing

3 Grace and peace to you from God our Father and the Lord Jesus Christ.

These aren't just nice words; there is power in a blessing! Notice that the Father and the Lord Jesus are distinct persons, but both have the power to grant grace and peace, which God alone possesses. Paul knows they will need that peace after reading this letter, and grace (God's unmerited favor) to put it into practice.

2

Corinth: The Good, the Bad, and the Ugly

1 Corinthians 1:4-17

The good: Thanksgiving for what God has done

Paul started most of his letters with thanksgiving. It is tempting to jump right in, point out the problem, and offer correction. You may have tried it with your wife. Hold on! First stop and think about what you can be thankful for in the relationship, and focus on the positive. It is a good example to follow with your spouse, family, and church!

[4] I always thank my God for you because of his grace given you in Christ Jesus. [5] For in him you have been enriched in every way— with all kinds of speech and with all knowledge — [6] God thus confirming our testimony about Christ among you. [7] Therefore you do not lack any spiritual gift as you eagerly wait for our Lord Jesus Christ to be revealed. [8] He will also keep you firm to the end, so that you will be blameless on the day of our Lord Jesus Christ. [9] God is faithful, who has called you into fellowship with his Son, Jesus Christ our Lord.

Paul packs a lot in one short paragraph!

- He always thanks God for them. Keep that same attitude of gratitude toward your imperfect family and church.
- They had a complicated and often difficult relationship, like that of many fathers and sons. Paul loved them, but agonized over their sin and rejection of his authority.
- We receive God's grace through relationship with Jesus.
- We are *in* Christ, united to him. God has enriched us through that intimate relationship. You have already been enriched in every way, in all kinds of speech and all knowledge. Do you feel rich? Discover and develop those tremendous riches! Don't run after worldly wealth!
- Their experience has confirmed what Paul preached to them about life in Christ, including spiritual gifts. Every spiritual gift was manifest! How about your church?
- They lived with the expectation of a coming kingdom, of Christ's return. Jesus is already present among us, but will be physically manifest when he returns. Are you eagerly awaiting his coming? Or is your life in this world so comfortable you really don't think much about it?
- Despite all their problems, Paul was confident that Jesus would keep them firm until the end. What a beautiful promise! Jesus is on your side! *Only* Jesus can keep you standing firm – you can't do it in your own strength.
- Jesus wants you to be blameless when he comes. He is at work right now preparing a spotless bride.
- Along with the call to holiness, they are called to fellowship with Jesus. Who we are, in relationship to God, is more important than what we do. How is your fellowship with Jesus?
- We may be unfaithful, but God is faithful.

The Bad: Divisions in the Church

You would think that with all these blessings everything would be fine. Not so. First, they are divided:

10 I appeal to you, brothers and sisters, in the name of our Lord Jesus Christ, that all of you agree with one another in what you say and that there be no divisions among you, but that you be perfectly united in mind and thought.

This is Paul's desire for every church:
- Harmony - all agreeing with one another
- No divisions among brothers and sisters
- Perfect unity
- Unity in mind (understanding)
- Unity in thought (purpose)

It sounds like Jesus' prayer in John 17, where he interceded for the *whole* church. Can you imagine the power of a worldwide church perfectly united in understanding and purpose?!

- Why do we act like it is impossible? Why are we suspicious of those who promote it?
- Do you share Paul's burden for church unity?
- What is the situation in your church?
- What are you doing to foster – or hinder – that unity, within your church and with other churches?

11 My brothers and sisters, some from Chloe's household have informed me that there are quarrels among you.

Informants! In prison they are called rats or snitches. Nobody likes them. The apostle or pastor needs to know what is going on in the church, but be careful!

- Discern the spirit of the person making the report.
- Watch for favoritism.
- Get reliable confirmation of what you are told.
- Discourage gossip.
- The church needs teaching on the proper way of dealing with sin they observe in their midst.

12 What I mean is this: One of you says, "I follow Paul"; another, "I follow Apollos"; another, "I follow Cephas"; still another, "I follow Christ." 13 Is Christ divided? Was Paul crucified for you? Were you baptized in the name of Paul?

May God free us from this rivalry! In most churches it runs rampant - among the worship team, deacon board, and elders. Who is the best preacher? Who prays with the most anointing? Who has the best voice?

Their divisions centered on the apostle they happened to follow, with the most "spiritual" saying they just followed Jesus. Isn't it the same today? We may follow Wesley, Luther, or Calvin. Many, who would never follow some long-dead theologian, are following a prophet, apostle, or TV preacher. It seems we are more man-centered and less united than ever!

It is tempting for successful preachers to promote this kind of near–idolatry, with TV shows, web sites, and schools named after them. It feels good when people say they go to "John Doe's" church. Don't take Jesus' place! It is *his* church! *His* body!

14 I thank God that I did not baptize any of you except Crispus and

Gaius, [15] *so no one can say that you were baptized in my name.* [16] *(Yes, I also baptized the household of Stephanas; beyond that, I don't remember if I baptized anyone else.)* [17] *For Christ did not send me to baptize, but to preach the gospel—not with wisdom and eloquence, lest the cross of Christ be emptied of its power.*

When we fill our preaching and books with human wisdom and eloquence, we empty the cross of its power. The Amplified Bible says it is *rendered vain - fruitless, void of value and of no effect.* It is amazing that we can have that ability! How do you think God feels about that? In the next chapter we will talk about how to preach with power.

Jesus didn't baptize, but he commanded us to. Paul knew he was not called to baptize, and he baptized very few. His co-workers, or local leaders, performed the baptisms, which was good, since it identified the new believers with Jesus instead of Paul. Avoid anything that brings undue attention to yourself.

The Ugly

Paul loves this church and is full of gratitude for all Christ has done in them, but his heart is heavy. He knows their divisions are quenching the Spirit, and that is just one of many serious problems. Beneath their super-spiritual façade, they are ugly. Most American churches are also confident, even smug. Could they be as ugly as Corinth?

1 Corinthians 1:18-31

18 For the message of the cross is foolishness to those who are perishing, but to us who are being saved it is the power of God. 19For it is written: "I will destroy the wisdom of the wise; the intelligence of the intelligent I will frustrate."

20 Where is the wise man? Where is the scholar? Where is the philosopher of this age? Has not God made foolish the wisdom of the world? 21For since in the wisdom of God the world through its wisdom did not know him, God was pleased through the foolishness of what was preached to save those who believe. 22 Jews demand miraculous signs and Greeks look for wisdom, 23but we preach Christ crucified: a stumbling block to Jews and foolishness to Gentiles, 24but to those whom God has called, both Jews and Greeks, Christ the power of God and the wisdom of God. 25For the foolishness of God is wiser than man's wisdom, and the weakness of God is stronger than man's strength.

26Brothers, think of what you were when you were called. Not many of you were wise by human standards; not many were influential; not many were of noble birth. 27But God chose the foolish things of the world to shame the wise; God chose the weak things of the world to shame the strong. 28He chose the lowly things of this world and the despised things—and the things that are not—to nullify the things that are, 29so that no one may boast before him. 30It is because of him that you are in Christ Jesus, who has become for us wisdom from God—that is, our righteousness, holiness and redemption. 31Therefore, as it is written: "Let him who boasts boast in the Lord."

3

The Foolishness of the Cross

1 Corinthians 1:18-31

Christians face a dilemma: Do we talk about the things that are foolishness to the world? Things which nobody wants to hear, like sin, repentance, holiness, and self-sacrifice? Or do we craft a message that pleases the world, emphasizing things like prosperity and happiness? To make the service exciting and relevant we add the latest technology, and music like the world's music. We want the world's wealth and all its toys. In the end it is hard to tell the difference between the church and the world.

God chooses the foolish, the weak, and the lowly

When Jesus walked this earth, not many wealthy, powerful, or religious people followed him. Didn't he say it is almost impossible for the rich to enter the kingdom (Matthew 19:23-24)? This chapter forces us to evaluate where we are at: *Brothers, think of what you were when you were called. Not many of you were wise by human standards; not many were influential; not many were of noble birth* (26). Today, many try to forget about their humble beginnings.

13

So what does God choose?

- *The foolish things of the world*
- *The weak things of the world*
- *The lowly things and the despised things*
- *The things that are not* (27-29)

That's strange! Why would God do that?

- *To shame the wise*
- *To shame the strong*
- *To nullify the things that are*
- *So that no one may boast before him* (also 27-29)

God's wisdom

Today we want wise men's approval. We want to be strong. We don't want to nullify the things that are - we want all their benefits! But it is far better to boast in the Lord Jesus! Look at the benefits for those who humble themselves to accept him:

- *Wisdom from God*
- *Righteousness (making us upright and putting us in right standing with God)*
- *Holiness (making us pure)*
- *Redemption (providing our ransom from the eternal penalty for sin)*
- *Being in (united to) Christ* (verse 30, Amplified)

Is it an accident that you don't hear many sermons about these things? They seem irrelevant in our sophisticated world. Many Christians don't even know what redemption means! Nobody wants to hear about holiness and righteousness. Preachers fear they will lose their people to churches that preach prosperity. We live in a world that overloads us with "wisdom" on the internet and thinks it knows everything! But God wants to *destroy the wisdom of the wise; and frustrate the intelligence of the intelligent* (19). The Amplified Bible makes it even clearer: *I will baffle and render useless and destroy the learning of the learned and the philosophy of the philosophers and the cleverness of the clever and the discernment of the discerning, I will frustrate and nullify them and bring them to nothing.*

Our world is full of advice on how to live. We won't say it, but many of us feel a little ashamed of the Bible and some of its teachings. It seems outdated. Maybe that is why you don't hear many sermons straight from the Bible. Some preachers make it worse by using Bibles with language hundreds of years old.

Christ crucified

The situation was the same in Paul's day. Jews were asking for signs, like many today who want miracles or some physical evidence that what we preach works. The world still seeks wisdom (22). Paul says: *Has not God made foolish the wisdom of the world?* (20) He does that by making sure it is impossible for the world to know God through its wisdom (21). That is why, even though he performed many miracles and taught great wisdom, Paul focused on the cross. For the lost (most of the world), that message is irrelevant foolishness. It is a stumbling block (23). But God's foolishness is wiser than man's wisdom, and God's weakness is stronger than man's strength (25).

May God give you eyes to see what is happening in your life and church. Our world needs Jesus more than ever. They need Christ crucified. They need the Christ of the Bible. Do we really believe what this passage teaches?
- God is still calling people (24).

- God still saves those who choose to believe the foolishness of the Gospel (21).
- The message of the cross is the power of God (18).
- For believers, the power of God and the wisdom of God is a person, the Lord Jesus Christ (24). It is not some elaborate system of living or all the technology this world offers, but an intimate relationship with the Son of God.

We have lost the power of the Gospel because we have bought into the world. We don't have to work up appearances of power, like so many try to. You will see God's power to save, deliver, and heal if you get back to the simple Gospel. We need revival. Preach the foolishness of the cross. For 2000 years it has unleashed God's power.

4

Paul Explodes Common Myths about Preaching
1 Corinthians 2:1-7, 14

¹When I came to you, brothers, I did not come with eloquence or superior wisdom as I proclaimed to you the testimony about God. ² For I resolved to know nothing while I was with you except Jesus Christ and him crucified. ³I came to you in weakness and fear, and with much trembling. ⁴My message and my preaching were not with wise and persuasive words, but with a demonstration of the Spirit's power, ⁵so that your faith might not rest on men's wisdom, but on God's power.

⁶We do, however, speak a message of wisdom among the mature, but not the wisdom of this age or of the rulers of this age, who are coming to nothing. ⁷No, we speak of God's secret wisdom, a wisdom that has been hidden and that God destined for our glory before time began. ¹⁴The man without the Spirit does not accept the things that come from the Spirit of God, for they are foolishness to him, and he cannot understand them, because they are spiritually discerned.

Was Paul a good preacher? Based on the number of people who came to Christ, the churches he established, and the lasting impact of his writings, it would be safe to assume he was. Yet this chapter seems to violate our concept of good preaching. Perhaps we have it wrong? Here are some common myths, and the reality according to Paul.

Myth: You must be confident, polished, and well-spoken.

Reality: *I came to you in weakness and fear, and with much trembling* (3).

The Amplified Bible makes it sound even worse: *I (passed into a state of) weakness and was in fear (dread) and great trembling.* It seems odd for Paul to experience that. Some have said it had to do with a physical ailment.

Are you ever afraid when you get up to preach or try to share the gospel with your neighbor? It's alright! Don't let that stop you! Just think about Paul trembling as he preached to the Corinthians!

Myth: There is so much competition among, mega-churches with great facilities, and great preachers on TV. I have to be really good or I will lose my people.

Reality: *My message and my preaching were not with wise and persuasive words, but with a demonstration of the Spirit's power* (4).

Of course it's good to prepare your message and communicate well, but even more important is a demonstration of the Spirit's power. All the messages recorded in Acts were very simple. Listen again to men like Billy Graham or Reinhard Bonnke. Their messages are simple, but there is a demonstration of the Spirit's power. We rely too much on interesting stories. There is too much power point and not enough power of the Spirit. Do your best, but above all, seek God's anointing so you preach with a demonstration of the Spirit's power. That may mean you don't look as impressive as the guys on TV, but it is the Spirit who changes lives. What do you really want?

Myth: We have to somehow work up faith so people can claim what they want from God.

Reality: Faith comes by hearing, and hearing by the Word of God. Paul was content being weak, so the Spirit could demonstrate his power, *so that your faith might not rest on man's wisdom, but on God's power* (5).

You can't have it both ways. Those who try to stir up faith that depends on human wisdom, drawing attention to themselves and speaking of the goodies people get through faith, are not preaching true faith. Paul didn't mind looking like a fool, trembling in front of the sophisticated Corinthians, because he wanted God to receive the glory. He wanted their faith to rest on God's power, not on himself. With our bands and smoke and drama and entertaining messages, there is little room left for the power of God.

Myth: Everyone knows the gospel. I have to bring some new revelation, something obscure from the Bible, if I am going to keep people in my church.

Reality: *I resolved to know nothing while I was with you except Jesus Christ and him crucified* (2).

And Paul knew a lot! Of course we can preach from the whole Bible, but the sad truth is that most preaching I hear today has very little Bible, and it doesn't seem to focus on Jesus. If we want power, we have to preach the pure Word, preach Christ, and preach the cross.

Having said that, Paul does have a message of wisdom for the mature, but it is not the world's wisdom that we hear so much of in the church. It is God's wisdom, which focuses on the Holy Spirit (6-7).

Myth: If I use hip words and make the gospel fit today's world, they will listen and receive it.

Reality: *The man without the Spirit does not accept the things that come from the Spirit of God, for they are foolishness to him, and he cannot understand them, because they are spiritually discerned* (14).

The preacher must work together with the Holy Spirit. Unless God opens their ears, we preach foolishness. That is why Jesus said so often: *"He who has ears to hear, let him hear."* Jesus' preaching was foolishness to many people. Some preach foolishness because they don't know what they are preaching, but if you are preaching the pure Word, don't worry if people don't receive it, or act like it is foolishness. Help your church experience the fullness of the Holy Spirit, so they can spiritually discern the truth.

5

More Than You Can Imagine

1 Corinthians 2:8-15

[8]None of the rulers of this age understood it, for if they had, they would not have crucified the Lord of glory. [9]However, as it is written:

"No eye has seen, no ear has heard, no mind has conceived what God has prepared for those who love him" — [10] but God has revealed it to us by his Spirit.

Don't trust your senses!

If you trust your eyes, ears, or mind, you are liable to do something like the political and religious leaders did around 30 AD: nail the Son of God to a cross and kill him. It doesn't excuse them, but Paul says they did it in ignorance. If they had only understood, they could never have committed such a horrendous act. And, incidentally, the necessary sacrifice for your sins would never have been offered. Aren't you glad God uses the things we do in ignorance? Have you ever acted foolishly? Perhaps you didn't understand your wife's feelings and killed her spirit with cruel words – or with silence. Or made a decision without fully understanding the implications – and hurt people, along with losing money and credibility.

You risk the same error in the spiritual realm. The brightest minds have gotten together to theologize on how the world is going to end, how God's absolute sovereignty rules out the possibility of falling away from Christ, or how the Scriptures they feel uncomfortable with no longer apply today. Instead of walking by faith we walk by sight, and end up full of fear and misjudging other people. We get into fights with the ones we love most because we respond to the angry words we hear, instead of listening to the heart.

If you rely on your intellect and senses, you are going to have a hard time with First Corinthians - and with the Christian life.

Three foundational truths in this passage:

1. God has prepared something beyond comprehension – for you!

2. There is a condition to receiving it: you must love him. After all, that is the first and greatest commandment. The Amplified Bible says it is those *who hold Him in affectionate reverence, promptly obeying Him and gratefully recognizing the benefits He has bestowed*. The word Paul uses here for love is agape: God-like, unconditional love. He may have been thinking about *those who wait for [God]* and *gladly do right, who remember his ways*, which is the context of his quote from Isaiah 64:4. Would you say you love God? How can you be sure? Jesus said if you love him, you will do what he asks you to do. Like your wife: If you repeatedly write off her desires or refuse to do something dear to her heart, how much do you really love her?

3. What God has prepared is not widely known; we only become aware of it through the Spirit's revelation.

Do you find it exciting and encouraging that God has something so amazing prepared for you? Are you curious to find out what it is?

[10]The Spirit searches all things, even the deep things of God. [11]For who among men knows the thoughts of a man except the man's spirit within him? In the same way no one knows the thoughts of God except the Spirit of God. [12] We have not received the spirit of the world but the Spirit who is from God, that we may understand what God has freely given us.

God gives you understanding!

They crucified Jesus because they lacked understanding - but the Spirit of God gives you that understanding! Jesus said: *the Holy Spirit, whom the Father will send in my name, will teach you all things; he will guide you into all the truth* (John 14:26; 16:13). You now have the inside track to discern God's very thoughts! That is better than all the intelligence that the government and technology companies have on us! Can you fathom the benefits of knowing God's thoughts? Thinking like he thinks? Seeing things from his perspective? Knowing what to do in any situation?

Throughout history there have always been some who claimed special, secret knowledge about God. That has resulted in many cults, like Gnosticism in the early church. But here we are told that the Spirit reveals even the very deepest things about God to any believer. We know that God loves to reveal himself: in creation, Scripture, and Jesus Christ. It makes sense that if he adopts you as a son he would also draw you into his inner circle and share his heart with you. The Spirit gives knowledge - but also the understanding and wisdom to correctly use it. God loves to give, and will freely give you everything he knows you are able to handle.

There is one other huge benefit for the Spirit-filled believer: The Spirit searches *all* things. He knows what is going on inside *everyone*. He certainly won't let you tap into their thoughts for your selfish purposes, or to satisfy your curiosity. But there is no reason to think he won't give you insight and discernment when you are praying about marrying someone, or considering a business deal. It can be baffling to try and figure out what is going on inside a person, but as you walk intimately with the Spirit, he gives you spiritual eyes to see their heart.

13This is what we speak, not in words taught us by human wisdom but in words taught by the Spirit, expressing spiritual truths in spiritual words. 14The man without the Spirit does not accept the things that come from the Spirit of God, for they are foolishness to him, and he cannot understand them, because they are spiritually discerned.

God teaches you how to speak

Have you ever gotten in trouble because you said something stupid? The old "foot in mouth" syndrome? Who hasn't? The Bible speaks extensively about the trouble our tongues cause and how hard they are to control. In addition to helping you discern God's thoughts, the Spirit can teach you how to speak! At first that will probably involve consciously evaluating what you are saying, to see if it is more in line with human wisdom, or with God's heart. Hopefully, as you walk in the Spirit, his words will become part of you. It can take time, because so much of our speech is untruthful, self-serving, and manipulative.

Unfortunately, when you speak this way, some people won't understand you, or may think you are crazy. There are even people in church who lack spiritual discernment and may not accept what you say. Their response to spiritual truth may provide insight into where they are at with God, although you don't want to write people off as not having the Spirit just because they don't agree with you. It is important to let the Spirit search your own heart and reveal your inner thoughts.

[15]*The spiritual man makes judgments about all things, but he himself is not subject to any man's judgment.*

The spiritual man makes judgments

What does it mean that you are *"not subject to any man's judgment?"* Paul is probably referring primarily to unbelievers' inability to make right judgments, since they don't have God's Spirit. As you walk closely with the Lord, you won't be as troubled by others' opinions, because what really matters is God's judgment of you. But be careful of being so "spiritual" that you arrogantly resist a brother's God-given correction, or ignore his "judgment" because you are "not subject to their judgment." The spiritual man also has a humble, submissive, heart, and welcomes correction.

Judging is widely misunderstood. Most people are familiar with Jesus' saying: *Judge not that you not be judged* (Matthew 7:1-2), but later in this same letter Paul talks about judging believers, in preparation for judging angels and others in eternity! There is a difference between making judgments and being judgmental. The spiritual man is alert to other people and situations, and needs to make righteous judgments about them. The Amplified Bible further clarifies: *he examines, investigates, inquires into, questions, and discerns all things.* Just avoid arrogantly setting yourself up as judge and acting like you are above everyone else because you are so spiritual!

[16] *"For who has known the mind of the Lord that he may instruct him?" But we have the mind of Christ.*

You have the mind of Christ

There is one last jewel in this chapter, whose importance could almost be overlooked. You have been offered insights into God's very thoughts through his indwelling Spirit, but now Paul says you actually *have the mind of Christ.* It comes in response to a question (*"who has known the mind of the Lord?"*) to which we would tend to answer "nobody." But Paul amazes us by saying that, in reality, we *can* know his mind! It is part of being one with Christ, having his Spirit dwelling in us, and abiding in him. It makes sense then that we would also have his mind, his understanding, and his insights into everything. If you can actually have Christ's mind, what more could you ask for?

Paul started this passage by suggesting that we can't know what God has prepared for us. I have heard many preachers say he is talking about heaven, and I am sure there is some of that, but Paul doesn't leave it there. He says you *can* know - God has revealed it to you by his Spirit. God has all this for you right now, for those who are truly Spirit-filled:
- The mind of Christ.
- The ability to make right judgments about all things.
- Transformed speech in words taught by the Spirit.
- Knowing God's very thoughts.

How tragic that many, just like the religious leaders that crucified Christ, lack this basic understanding of what God has provided for us.

1 Corinthians 3

¹Brothers, I could not address you as spiritual but as worldly—mere infants in Christ. ²I gave you milk, not solid food, for you were not yet ready for it. Indeed, you are still not ready. ³You are still worldly. For since there is jealousy and quarreling among you, are you not worldly? Are you not acting like mere men? ⁴For when one says, "I follow Paul," and another, "I follow Apollos," are you not mere men?

⁵What, after all, is Apollos? And what is Paul? Only servants, through whom you came to believe—as the Lord has assigned to each his task. ⁶I planted the seed, Apollos watered it, but God made it grow. ⁷So neither he who plants nor he who waters is anything, but only God, who makes things grow. ⁸The man who plants and the man who waters have one purpose, and each will be rewarded according to his own labor. ⁹For we are God's fellow workers; you are God's field, God's building.

¹⁰By the grace God has given me, I laid a foundation as an expert builder, and someone else is building on it. But each one should be careful how he builds. ¹¹For no one can lay any foundation other than the one already laid, which is Jesus Christ. ¹²If any man builds on this foundation using gold, silver, costly stones, wood, hay or straw, ¹³his work will be shown for what it is, because the Day will bring it to light. It will be revealed with fire, and the fire will test the quality of each man's work. ¹⁴If what he has built survives, he will receive his reward. ¹⁵If it is burned up, he will suffer loss; he himself will be saved, but only as one escaping through the flames.

¹⁶Don't you know that you yourselves are God's temple and that God's Spirit lives in you? ¹⁷If anyone destroys God's temple, God will destroy him; for God's temple is sacred, and you are that temple.

¹⁸Do not deceive yourselves. If any one of you thinks he is wise by the standards of this age, he should become a "fool" so that he may become wise. ¹⁹For the wisdom of this world is foolishness in God's sight. As it is written: "He catches the wise in their craftiness"; ²⁰and again, "The Lord knows that the thoughts of the wise are futile." ²¹So then, no more boasting about men! All things are yours, ²²whether Paul or Apollos or Cephas or the world or life or death or the present or the future—all are yours, ²³and you are of Christ, and Christ is of God.

6

Will You Enter Heaven as one Escaping through the Flames?
1 Corinthians 3

Paul uses two metaphors to describe the church:

1. A field

- In a field, some plant, others water. In the church, God has assigned different people to each task. In this case, Paul sowed while Apollos watered (6).
- Everyone has to do their part if we are to have a harvest. We are all working for the same purpose. A pastor, for example, is not better than another church member; they simply have different work in the field (8).
- We have the great privilege of being fellow workers with God. (9).
- God knows your abilities and assigns each one their task (5). He doesn't ask for volunteers. We are in rebellion if we don't do our assigned part, and the harvest will be affected. The most important task belongs to God: he makes it grow (6).
- If God is not at work, you can plant the best seed and

water and feed it all day long, but you won't get a harvest.

- The harvest is very important to God; that is the purpose of the field. If it is not fruitful, it is worthless (John 15:6-8), but if we are abiding in Christ there should be a good harvest.

2. A building, or a temple

- Just as Paul sowed in the field, he lays the foundation of this building. He is an *"expert builder"* (10).
- Others then build on that foundation. To get a solid building, each one has to work carefully (10). If the foundation is bad, the whole building will be bad.
- The only foundation for a church is Jesus Christ. If the foundation is a pastor or doctrine, it is not a true church.

Things that can harm the field or building

1. Divisions

- It is common for Christians to identify with some theologian, apostle, church leader or denomination. To do so is to act like mere men (4).
- Following a man or doctrine produces jealousy and quarreling, and betrays immaturity (3).
- Instead of being spiritual, they are worldly infants (1).
- To be mature in Christ we hold onto solid doctrine, but put aside anything else that divides the church.

2. Using poor materials

- You can build with gold, silver, and costly stones. The best. Or you can use wood, hay, and straw (12). You can build on sand or on rock. For a while both buildings may look the same, but when storms come, the materials' quality will be revealed. The coming judgment will bring everything to light (13). Many are using poor materials to save money, time and energy. It is more costly to use the best, but the Lord's temple deserves it.

- Although it is not a salvation issue, the quality of your work will affect you for eternity. You will be saved, but only as one escaping through the flames (15). If your work is burned up, you will suffer loss (the Bible doesn't say what that will be). But if your work survives, you will receive a reward (14). Building the Lord's temple is serious business.

3. Underestimating the importance of the Church

- The church (the body of believers) is God's temple, even more important than the temple that stood in Jerusalem. It is sacred (17). Many don't regard the church that highly. Since it is God's temple, if someone destroys it, God will destroy them (17).

- How do we destroy the temple?
    - Not taking care of the sheep
    - False doctrine and lack of feeding from the Word
    - Quarrels and divisions
    - Sin and selfish ambition.

Don't play around with the church. Every church leader should have a healthy fear of God and take his job seriously.

In chapter six Paul says our bodies are also temples of the Spirit. Do you think God might also destroy the person who destroys his temple with gluttony, drugs, alcohol, cigarettes, or abuse?

Some things to reflect on from this chapter:

1. Am I mature? Or immature? What criteria do I use to determine if someone is worldly or spiritual? Can I confidently say I am not following a man or doctrine? That I am not contributing to quarrels, jealousy, or divisions in the church?

2. Am I giving solid food to believers who are still infants? Do I need to change what I am preaching to give more milk to the congregation? Or is my church ready for solid food? Am I giving it to them?

3. What can I do to heal divisions in the church?

4. What is my part in the Lord's field? Am I allowing God to make it grow? If it is not growing, why not? Am I allowing and encouraging others to do their part? Is it possible I am watering when no one has even sown?

5. Can I confidently say that Christ is the foundation of my life, family, and church? What would I have to change to give Christ that place?

6. Am I using the best in my service to the Lord? Does it appear my work will survive the test? Or is it already showing signs of strain under the pressures of this world? Is there something I

need to change so I won't suffer loss? *Better to put your work to the test now and prepare for the coming judgement.* Ask some brothers to help evaluate it.

7. Am I suffering because God is judging me for destroying a temple? How can I let others know how important the church is to God? What can I do if I see someone destroying God's temple?

1 Corinthians 4

¹So then, men ought to regard us as servants of Christ and as those entrusted with the secret things of God. ²Now it is required that those who have been given a trust must prove faithful. ³I care very little if I am judged by you or by any human court; indeed, I do not even judge myself. ⁴My conscience is clear, but that does not make me innocent. It is the Lord who judges me. ⁵Therefore judge nothing before the appointed time; wait till the Lord comes. He will bring to light what is hidden in darkness and will expose the motives of men's hearts. At that time each will receive his praise from God.

⁶Now, brothers, I have applied these things to myself and Apollos for your benefit, so that you may learn from us the meaning of the saying, "Do not go beyond what is written." Then you will not take pride in one man over against another. ⁷For who makes you different from anyone else? What do you have that you did not receive? And if you did receive it, why do you boast as though you did not?

⁸Already you have all you want! Already you have become rich! You have become kings— and that without us! How I wish that you really had become kings so that we might be kings with you! ⁹For it seems to me that God has put us apostles on display at the end of the procession, like men condemned to die in the arena. We have been made a spectacle to the whole universe, to angels as well as to men. ¹⁰We are fools for Christ, but you are so wise in Christ! We are weak, but you are strong! You are honored, we are dishonored! ¹¹To this very hour we go hungry and thirsty, we are in rags, we are brutally treated, we are homeless. ¹²We work hard with our own hands. When we are cursed, we bless; when we are persecuted, we endure it; ¹³ when we are slandered, we answer kindly. Up to this moment we have become the scum of the earth, the refuse of the world.

¹⁴I am not writing this to shame you, but to warn you, as my dear children. ¹⁵Even though you have ten thousand guardians in Christ, you do not have many fathers, for in Christ Jesus I became your father through the gospel. ¹⁶Therefore I urge you to imitate me. ¹⁷For this reason I am sending to you Timothy, my son whom I love, who is faithful in the Lord. He will remind you of my way of life in Christ Jesus, which agrees with what I teach everywhere in every church.

¹⁸Some of you have become arrogant, as if I were not coming to you. ¹⁹But I will come to you very soon, if the Lord is willing, and then I will find out not only how these arrogant people are talking, but what power they have. ²⁰For the kingdom of God is not a matter of talk but of power. ²¹What do you prefer? Shall I come to you with a whip, or in love and with a gentle spirit?

7

The Struggle of a Spiritual Father

1 Corinthians 4

This chapter gives us a glimpse of Paul's heart - full of love, pain, and longing for his spiritual children.

What grieves him most is their arrogance (8):

- *Already you have all you want!*
- *Already you have become rich!*
- *You have become kings - and that without us!*

They have arrived. They no longer need anybody or anything. They are wealthy and happy, and think they are spiritually mature, but they are blind to some serious problems in their church. They remind me of the church at Laodicea in Revelation 3:17: "*You say 'I am rich; I have acquired wealth and do not need a thing.' But you do not realize that you are wretched, pitiful, poor, blind, and naked.*"

In their own eyes, the Corinthians are:

- *Wise*
- *Strong*

35

- *Honored* (10)

Yet Paul says that apostles, whom we assume would be examples of a godly life, are:

- *Fools* (to those lacking spiritual discernment)
- *Weak* (in the world's eyes)
- *Dishonored*
- *Hungry*
- *Thirsty*
- *In rags*
- *Brutally treated*
- *Homeless*
- *Hard workers with their own hands*
- *Cursed - but they bless*
- *Persecuted - but they endure it*
- *Slandered - but they answer kindly*
- *The scum of the earth, the refuse of the world* (10-12)

Today many want to call themselves apostles. Be careful! An apostle is a very serious and difficult calling. *"God has put us apostles on display at the end of the procession, like men condemned to die in the arena."* Instead of the glory some seek as apostles, *"We have been made a spectacle to the whole universe, to angels as well as to men" (9).*

Why would God allow a faithful servant to suffer so much? Was it because Paul wasn't that great an apostle? Or could it be that today's "apostles" don't really understand what it means to be an apostle?

The heart of a spiritual father

The father heart of an apostle suffers as he sees his son hurting. Paul never had his own children, but he had many spiritual children. We may have thousands of guardians (or tutors, verse 15), in Christ, but we have only one father who birthed us in the gospel. Do you have contact with your spiritual father? Do you give him the honor he deserves?

We have all heard the saying "Do as I say, not as I do," but that is hypocritical. More important than instruction is a father's good example. To know and follow that example means spending time together, like the intensive time the disciples spent with Jesus. You know nothing about the daily life of someone you see on TV or the internet. The Corinthians knew Paul, and he is sending one of his most beloved sons (Timothy) to remind them of his way of life (17).

Paul speaks this way because they must recognize his authority if they are to receive his correction. He can deal with the suffering that comes from being an apostle if he knows that his children (in this case in Corinth), are receiving his teaching and growing in Christ. Paul could care less about money or recognition - he longs for their well-being. As an apostle called by Jesus he is obligated to speak the truth, or he would be in sin and rebellion.

Some misunderstand Paul. They don't appreciate the heart of a spiritual father. Paul modeled sacrificial love, as any father should, so he is able to say: "*I urge you to follow my example, to imitate me.*" *(16)*

I pray for consistency in your life and teaching (17), that you would have someone you can imitate, and that your life would be a good example to many.

8

How to Respond to Sin in the Church
1 Corinthians 5

Are you aware of sin in your church? Does anyone seem to care? Do you know what to do about it? Do you feel like it is not any of your business? This is a hard chapter, because it shows how far we have strayed from the example of the early church. This is the first of two cases (the other is in the next chapter) of sin in the church and how to deal with it.

Are you your brother's keeper?

[1] It is actually reported that there is sexual immorality among you, and of a kind that does not occur even among pagans: A man has his father's wife. [2] And you are proud! Shouldn't you rather have been filled with grief and have put out of your fellowship the man who did this?

In the prison culture I knew for many years, a "rat" (someone who informed the officers of a violation) was hated. Most believers today probably think someone else's sin is none of their business, but you are your brother's keeper (Genesis 4:9). Some secretly rejoice when a brother stumbles, because it makes them look more spiritual, but our first reaction should be to grieve over what has happened (2). Out of love for the person, and concern for God's holiness and the testimony of the church, we are compelled to act. The whole body suffers because of one member's sin. Are you so used to seeing sin that it doesn't bother you? Do you realize how important God's holiness is?

The Corinthians ignored the sin. Their leaders were so out of touch they were proud and even boastful about their church despite the sin. In many large churches today we don't even know what is going on in our brothers' lives. If we do see something, the tendency is to ignore it, gossip about it, or perhaps (if we are really spiritual) pray about it. Most church leaders seem to lack the boldness, anointing, and knowledge to deal with it.

Jesus said it is not only the leader's responsibility, but the responsibility of every believer. He gave us a model of how to deal with a brother who sins (or, as some manuscripts say, sins against us) in Matthew 18:

1. Find the brother and speak to him in private.
2. If he doesn't listen, go with one or two witnesses.
3. If he still won't listen, bring it before the church.

The role of the apostle

Paul honored Jesus' teaching and applied it to the church. He knew sin must be dealt with, and since the Corinthians ignored the sin, it became his responsibility as an apostle to confront it. Verse 3 gives us a glimpse of how apostolic authority functions:

3 Even though I am not physically present, I am with you in spirit.

And I have already passed judgment on the one who did this, just as if I were present.

The church is not a business or a club. It is a supernatural manifestation of the Body of Christ. So *"I am with you in spirit"* is not just a nice saying; Paul believes that on a spiritual level he is actually present. That is powerful! Authority functions outside our concept of time and space. It was that understanding which amazed Jesus when the centurion said: *"I do not deserve to have you come under my roof...but say the word, and my servant will be healed. For I myself am a man under authority."* Jesus never came near his house, but spiritually he was present there, and the servant was healed (Luke 7:1-10).

Like a child when his parents are away, the Corinthians thought they could get away with their sin, but Paul says "Sorry, I am right there with you:" *I have already passed judgment on the one who did this, just as if I were present.* An apostle can, and must, judge sin in a church under his supervision. To do so he needs to know what is going on, and the boldness to act. Something happens in the Spirit when he makes that judgment.

The church's role

Paul has done his part, but now, under his apostolic authority, the church must do theirs. There are three crucial conditions which have to be met before they act:

[4] When you are assembled in the name of our Lord Jesus and I am with you in spirit, and the power of our Lord Jesus is present, [5] hand this man over to Satan, so that the sinful nature may be destroyed and his spirit saved on the day of the Lord.

1. *Be assembled in the name of our Lord Jesus*

This involves more than ending an opening prayer with "In Jesus' name." By faith in Jesus' words (*"where two or more are gathered in my name there I am in the midst of them"*) we believe that Jesus himself is in the service. Significantly, that is in the same passage where he speaks of the power of unity, and dealing with brothers who sin against us (Matthew 18:15-20).

2. *The power of our Lord Jesus is present*

It would be dangerous to discipline the brother if Jesus' power were not present. Apparently having Jesus there doesn't automatically mean his power is there - sometimes we need to wait, or confess sin, before we can experience it. How often is the power of Jesus truly present in our services? How would you determine if it were present or not? If there is no power it is not surprising that people are caught up in sin.

3. *Paul is with them in spirit*

Neither Paul nor the church does this on their own; they work together. Paul's presence gives them the authority; they need the faith to believe that Paul is present.

If the person does not receive the correction

Only if these conditions are met, and the person in unrepentant despite doing everything possible to help him, ***hand this man over to Satan, so that the sinful nature may be destroyed and his spirit saved on the day of the Lord*** (5).

It is clear there is a dynamic here that most of us never experience in church. Only under these conditions could they do something as radical as hand a brother over to Satan.

1. It is not punishment or revenge, but loving discipline, with the goal of restoring the brother. Every church needs safeguards to avoid possible abuses.

2. The sinful nature must be destroyed, and in this case that is not the Spirit's work, but Satan's! This seems to dismiss the excuse that we will always struggle with the flesh. The Romans 7 experience is a life without the power of the Spirit. If that fleshly sinful nature is not destroyed, his spirit will not be saved! Think about the implications of that statement! Is the sinful nature alive and well in you? Or has it been destroyed? We cannot allow for any accommodation to the flesh. It must be crucified! Better to be obedient and crucify your own flesh than be handed over to Satan to have it destroyed.

3. How is it destroyed? The man is now out from under the church's covering and vulnerable to Satan's attacks - physically, emotionally, and spiritually. The purpose is the destruction of the flesh, not the whole person, even though at times they may die (like Ananias and Saphira in Acts 5, see also 1 Corinthians 11:30).

4. The only other example of handing someone over to Satan is in 1 Timothy 1:19-20. Some had *"shipwrecked their faith"* by not holding on to *"faith and a good conscience"*, so Paul handed them over to Satan *"to be taught not to blaspheme."* This is obviously not something done hastily or lightly. Much prayer and great

care is needed or terrible damage can be done!

Why is it so important to deal with sin in the church and exercise this discipline?

⁶ Your boasting is not good. Don't you know that a little yeast works through the whole batch of dough? ⁷ Get rid of the old yeast that you may be a new batch without yeast—as you really are. For Christ, our Passover lamb, has been sacrificed. ⁸ Therefore let us keep the Festival, not with the old yeast, the yeast of malice and wickedness, but with bread without yeast, the bread of sincerity and truth.

First of all, it affects his eternal salvation, but even worse is the potentially devastating impact on the whole church. Verse six says a little yeast works through the whole batch of dough. Remember Acan in Joshua seven? One man's sin brought defeat to the whole nation. One person in sin will act like a cancer in the whole body. The old yeast of malice and wickedness is to be put aside in favor of the bread of sincerity and truth.

So how are we to relate to sinners – in the church and in the world?

The final verses of this chapter show how they (and many of us) had things backward:

⁹ I have written you in my letter not to associate with sexually immoral people— ¹⁰ not at all meaning the people of this world who are immoral, or the greedy and swindlers, or idolaters. In that case you would have to leave this world. ¹¹ But now I am writing you that you must not associate with anyone who calls himself a brother but is sexually immoral or greedy, an idolater or a slanderer, a drunkard or a swindler. With such a man do not even eat.

[12] What business is it of mine to judge those outside the church? Are you not to judge those inside? [13] God will judge those outside. "Expel the wicked man from among you."

A Christian is not to associate with sexually immoral people, or even eat with them! Nothing! But there was a big misunderstanding about what he meant. Paul is not talking about people in the world. If that were the case, you would have to leave this world! Many Christians would like to – and have attempted to. But we are the salt of the earth and the light of the world! The immoral, greedy, swindlers, and idolaters need us! Jesus was a *"friend of tax collectors and sinners"* (Matthew 11:19). Follow his example and befriend them! Many Christians, like the Pharisees, want nothing to do with them, but it is not our job to judge those outside the church (12). That is for God to do! Be careful of usurping his job!

The problem is not the world – it is the church! Verse 11 says: *You must not associate with anyone **who calls himself a brother** but is*:

- Sexually immoral: Can you imagine if we took this seriously and stopped associating with anyone in church who was engaged in pornography, sex out of marriage, or some other sexual sin?
- Greedy: There goes a big part of the church! No covetousness or greed is allowed.
- An Idolater: An idol is anything that takes first place in your life, time, and attention, other than God. Think

money, computers, TV, pleasure...

- A Slanderer: Gossips; those who put down the pastor and others in the church or just have a bad mouth.
- A Drunkard: How much do you have to drink to be a drunkard?
- A Swindler: Anyone dishonest in their business, taxes, or little things in daily life.

Don't even eat with them (11)!

God will take care of those outside the church. It is the Christian's job to judge those inside. But it seems impossible! We would lose half the church! As with discipline, great care is needed here.

Guidance on discipline

1. We are talking about the person who is *practicing* sin. We all sin at times. I John 1:8 says: *If we say we have no sin we deceive ourselves and the truth is not in us.*

2. This person is hardened, covering up his sin, or sinning openly, because he really doesn't care. He acts like he doesn't have to answer to anyone. God wants us to have a broken, repentant heart, that goes running to God when we sin, seeking his mercy and forgiveness.

3. Only after having done everything possible to help the "sinner" are we commanded to expel the wicked person (verse 13, Deuteronomy 17:7). The Old Testament was really tough on sin – many would get stoned or cast out to keep the community sin-free.

But isn't it almost impossible to put the teaching in this chapter into practice?

I know the excuses:

- "Paul doesn't really expect us to do this."
- "That is impossible today. That was just for the early church. "
- "We would be in court all the time and in trouble with the authorities."
- "We will lose our whole church!"
- "They will call us fanatics."

To be honest, I am tired of the excuses, and I suspect that God is. The church is full of bad yeast which has infected the whole body. We don't know what Jesus' power is all about. He doesn't even show up in many of our services, there is so much sin there. We don't preach about sin, repentance, or holiness. We resist the authority of an apostle, pastor, or church. We are rebels who don't want to give up our sin. If we do try to put this into practice, people will just go to a church that's more "loving" and "accepting" which doesn't "judge." But it is not for us to take out parts of the Bible we don't agree with, or that appear outdated. As in all of the Christian life, God will help us obey it.

The key teachings in this passage:

1. The importance of authority. By nature we are rebellious and resist authority. It has been rejected in the home, school, and society, and the same rebellion has filled the church. Every believer should be under the authority of a church, and every

church under ecclesiastical authority, which is under Christ's authority. When we break that chain of authority we lose the power of the Spirit. There have been many abuses of authority, but that doesn't mean we just give up on it.

2. We are also under the Bible's authority. There is right and wrong. It is not up to us to decide what is permissible or not. Christ died because of our sin, and we make light of that sacrifice when we take sin lightly.

3. We are in the world, but not of the world. There should be an obvious difference between the church and the world.

4. Church discipline is not optional. We must deal with sin in the church.

May God have mercy on us! May the blood of Jesus purify us! May we repent of our sin and our tolerance of sin! We are ripe for God's judgment! More than ever we need the Spirit's fullness to guide us and counsel us on these sensitive issues.

9

Judges in the Church?
1 Corinthians 6:1-11

In the previous chapter Paul talked about judging sin in the church: "*Are you not to judge those inside?*" (5:12) I know that goes against the grain. We feel uncomfortable with it. Any attempt to obey Paul's command here will be met with a chorus of "you're being judgmental." Indeed, we have to balance it with what Jesus said, as in Matthew 7:1-5:

> *"Do not judge, or you too will be judged. For in the same way you judge others, you will be judged, and with the measure you use, it will be measured to you. "Why do you look at the speck of sawdust in your brother's eye and pay no attention to the plank in your own eye? How can you say to your brother, 'Let me take the speck out of your eye,' when all the time there is a plank in your own eye? You hypocrite, first take the plank out of your own eye, and then you will see clearly to remove the speck from your brother's eye."*

Read it carefully. Jesus is speaking here of someone with a critical spirit, blind to his own faults, looking for reasons to accuse his brother. However, the last verse specifically grants permission to remove a speck from a brother's eye! The requirement is to see clearly so we won't hurt him. To have that clarity we must first remove the log from our own eye and get our lives in order.

Jesus laid the foundation and Paul affirms it: We should judge those inside the church. Does that seem strange or too radical? Does it go against your experience in church? We have already seen in this letter how much we have lost of what Christ intended for the church. Are we going to do what the Word of God says to do?

Yes, judge we must. In chapter five it was a case of sexual sin. Now Paul moves to lawsuits among believers:

¹If any of you has a dispute with another, dare he take it before the ungodly for judgment instead of before the saints? ² Do you not know that the saints will judge the world? And if you are to judge the world, are you not competent to judge trivial cases? ³ Do you not know that we will judge angels? How much more the things of this life! ⁴ Therefore, if you have disputes about such matters, appoint as judges even men of little account in the church! ⁵ I say this to shame you. Is it possible that there is nobody among you wise enough to judge a dispute between believers? ⁶ But instead, one brother goes to law against another—and this in front of unbelievers!

⁷ The very fact that you have lawsuits among you means you have been completely defeated already. Why not rather be wronged? Why not rather be cheated? ⁸ Instead, you yourselves cheat and do wrong, and you do this to your brothers.

The sin at Corinth

- They cheat and wrong their own brothers! (6:8)
- They take problems among Christians before unbelievers in secular courts (6).
- They are trusting the world to resolve issues in the Body of Christ.

Paul's more basic questions is: Why are Christians even having lawsuits?

- He says they are "*completely defeated already*" (7).
- A Christian should not be suing another Christian.
- They should be able to work things out among themselves.
- Instead of suing and going to court, they may need to accept being wronged (7).

Jesus said (Matthew 5:39-40): *"Do not resist an evil person. If someone strikes you on the right cheek, turn to him the other also. And if someone wants to sue you and take your tunic, let him have your cloak as well..."*

We are quick to claim our right. Sadly, conflicts are common in most churches, and we do not receive much help from the leadership to resolve them.

How to deal with lawsuits among believers:

The Christian should live in peace with his brothers, but we are human and will have conflicts at times. The church needs to help resolve them without involving unbelievers.

The process? Appoint judges from the brothers of the church (4-5). The Greek is not totally clear: Is Paul saying they are naming men of little account, and that is wrong? Or does he mean that even a brother of little account is able to serve as judge? Either way, the message is: There are men in the church who are wise enough to appoint as judges. He doesn't elaborate on the process, but as with everything we do in the church, it must be under the anointing and direction of the Holy Spirit. If we try to do it in the flesh it certainly will prove disastrous.

When was the last time you saw "judges" in a church? Who would you go to in your church if you had a serious problem with another brother? Notice again the church's active role in members' lives. It doesn't ignore problems, but confronts them and resolves them, while maintaining a good testimony before the world. How sad to see division and hatred among brothers go unresolved for years!

Judges in the Old Testament

It may be that Paul, with his great knowledge of the Law, was thinking about what Jethro suggested to his son-in-law in the desert, which Moses put into practice:

> *"Teach them his decrees and instructions, and show them the way they are to live and how they are to behave. But select capable men from all the people—men who fear God, trustworthy men who hate dishonest gain—and appoint them as officials over thousands, hundreds, fifties and tens. Have them serve as judges for the people at all times, but have them bring every difficult case to you; the simple cases they can*

decide themselves. That will make your load lighter, because they will share it with you. If you do this and God so commands, you will be able to stand the strain, and all these people will go home satisfied" (Exodus 18:20-23).

- It was Moses' responsibility to teach God's Word to the people. Biblical knowledge is fundamental to our right conduct. Many problems would be avoided if the whole church were well instructed in the Bible. That is the responsibility of the pastor and other leaders in the church.

- In this case it was up to Moses to appoint the judges. They had to be:
  - Capable (competent)
  - God-fearing
  - Trustworthy (men of truth)
  - Haters of dishonest gain

  Not that different from the qualities of elders and deacons in the church (1 Timothy 3:1-16, Titus 1:6-9).

- There were various levels of judges, and they served full-time. Since this was for the entire nation, that makes sense. They were over groups of one thousand, one hundred, fifty, and ten. We can assume that most cases could be resolved at the first level, but the person could appeal to the next level, or the judge could refer a difficult case to the next level. The hardest ones were brought to Moses. Something similar could work in the church, with leaders of small groups or home groups at the first level. In a large church it could be necessary for some to work full-time.

- When people fell they are heard and cared for, we avoid many problems, it takes stress off the leaders, and the people go home satisfied.

Two important points in this passage:

1. God trusts us to judge.
- Believers are going to judge the world (2). Possibly Paul was thinking of Daniel 7:22:
- We are also going to judge angels.
- If we are able to do that, surely we are able to judge cases in the church. In fact, God uses the problems in the church and our daily life to train us for the future.
- The example of Moses and Israel could guide us.

2. It is a total contradiction for believers to live in sin.

⁹ Do you not know that the wicked will not inherit the kingdom of God? Do not be deceived: Neither the sexually immoral nor idolaters nor adulterers nor male prostitutes nor homosexual offenders ¹⁰ nor thieves nor the greedy nor drunkards nor slanderers nor swindlers will inherit the kingdom of God. ¹¹ And that is what some of you were. But you were washed, you were sanctified, you were justified in the name of the Lord Jesus Christ and by the Spirit of our God.

The wicked will not inherit the kingdom of God. Some examples of the wicked (not an inclusive list):

- Sexually immoral

- Idolaters
- Adulterers
- Male prostitutes
- Homosexuals
- Thieves
- The greedy
- Drunkards
- Slanderers
- Swindlers

Those are troubling verses, but most of those practices are common – even accepted – today. We shouldn't condemn them; Jesus came to save them and set them free from their sins. We all were sinners, and these are not unpardonable sins. A Christian can sin, repent, and be forgiven. But the word is very clear: it is not possible to *continue* committing these sins, *practicing* them on a regular basis, and be saved and enter the kingdom of God.

When we accept Christ we are:

- Washed.
- Sanctified (separated from the world, set apart for a purpose).
- Justified (declared "not guilty," just as if we had never sinned).

How can we go back and live in sin?

Many have been deceived into thinking they have their ticket to heaven and can live as they wish. There is a lot of pressure to accept them in the church, especially those in sexual sin, which Paul addresses in the second part of this chapter.

Jesus came to wash you and free you from sin. There is no sin (except blasphemy of the Holy Spirit) that he cannot forgive. He wants to justify you; declare you "not guilty." If you have accepted Christ and are living in sin, don't wait. Repent right now and ask his forgiveness.

10

Sanctified Sexuality
1 Corinthians 6:12-20

I have ministered to thousands of men over the past forty years: single and married, pastor and prisoner, young and old. Most don't talk much about it, but they all struggle with sex. Temptations may change over time, but it is still real for the ninety-year-old. It is a leading cause of pastors' downfalls. Pornography has always been a temptation, but with the internet it has become a cancer in the church. Some studies say 40% of *pastors* are trapped in internet porn.

God is very interested in your sex life. After all, sex was his idea. He made you a man. Jesus knows what it's like to be a man; he was tempted just like you are –and never sinned. He is your high priest who can - and wants to - help you. Talk with God about your struggles. He already knows anyway. Don't separate your spiritual and sexual life.

The Bible talks openly about sex. Song of Solomon celebrates it. In Ephesians 5:31-32 Paul compares the sexual union of a man and woman to the relationship of Christ and the church. The mystery of two people becoming one flesh reflects the mystery of the God-head - three persons in one. That is why Satan works overtime to pervert and destroy sex. Ephesians 5:3 says that the Christian should not even *mention* sexual immorality or impurity.

The sad reality is that many Christian men think and talk about sex all day. They fill their minds with impurity on the TV and internet. It is a hard struggle, but you can overcome the temptation. The Bible chronicles many men's struggles and failures. Sexual sin was a big problem in Rome and Greece, and had invaded the church, as we saw in chapter five. Some of the clearest biblical teaching on sex is found in this passage.

For any ladies reading this, there are plenty of principles that apply to women as well. This may help you understand the man in your life, but be aware I write frankly, to help your brothers.

What the passage teaches

[12] *"Everything is permissible for me"—but not everything is beneficial. "Everything is permissible for me"—but I will not be mastered by anything.*

1. We are free in Christ. Some things are not specifically prohibited, but are they beneficial? Do they help me be the man God wants me to be?

2. Some things which are permissible can easily master and control us, and thus become sin.

[13] *"Food for the stomach and the stomach for food"—but God will destroy them both. The body is not meant for sexual immorality, but for the Lord, and the Lord for the body.*

3. God made each part of the body for a purpose. Your body is not for you to abuse as you wish. Your body is meant for the Lord and should be used as he intended.

14 By his power God raised the Lord from the dead, and he will raise us also.

4. Sex is only for this life – in heaven we will be sex-less, like the angels (see Matthew 22:30). We might think, "And that's paradise?", but God knows what he's doing!

15 Do you not know that your bodies are members of Christ himself? Shall I then take the members of Christ and unite them with a prostitute? Never!

5. Think carefully about what you are doing with your body; it is a member of Christ.

16 Do you not know that he who unites himself with a prostitute is one with her in body? For it is said, "The two will become one flesh."

6. No matter who it is, when you have sex with someone, you become one flesh with them.

17 But he who unites himself with the Lord is one with him in spirit.

7. There is a parallel between the union of a man and woman, and the union of Christ and the believer.

18 Flee from sexual immorality. All other sins a man commits are outside his body, but he who sins sexually sins against his own body.

8. We are commanded to flee sexual immorality. God doesn't command us to do something without empowering us to do it.

The problem many times is that we don't want to flee; we would rather jump right in.

9. There is something unique about sexual sin – it touches the deepest part of a man. It is a sin against your own body.

    [19] Do you not know that your body is a temple of the Holy Spirit, who is in you, whom you have received from God? You are not your own; [20] you were bought at a price. Therefore honor God with your body.

10. Your body is a temple of the Holy Spirit. Honor God with your body.

11. Jesus bought you with the price of his blood – you are not your own.

Some applications

1. God's intention is for a man to have one woman for life. That is how we most fully experience being "one flesh". How is it possible to be "one flesh" with ten women?

-   Any sex outside the committed marital relationship is sin and robs us of the intimacy God desires us to have with our wives. That includes fantasies, masturbation, and pornography. It is impossible for gay sex to result in the intimacy and completion found in the restoration of the one-ness we had when God created us in his image.

-   Adultery was prohibited in the Ten Commandments, and the penalty was death.

- In this same chapter (verse 9) Paul said that those who continue in sexual sin and adultery cannot be saved.

- Instead of the freedom which some feel sexual experimentation gives, sexual sin destroys the power and meaning of the sexual union.

- If you really love your wife, prove it by fighting sexual temptation. You will reap great benefits in your intimate relationship with her.

2. Many men live under great condemnation because they can't overcome masturbation. It is not the worst sin. The Bible never mentions masturbation by name, but there are many Biblical principles we can apply:

- It is not beneficial. It leaves you empty and far from God. It is easy to be mastered by masturbation.

- It stimulates a man to think more about sex, have fantasies, and view pornography. God may give wet dreams to provide sexual release, if needed. Think about this as you consider masturbating: Am I honoring God? Do I feel right doing this with a member of Christ?

- You can live without sex. Christ did. The testimony of many single men, soldiers, prisoners, and others without a wife available is that life is much easier if you are not constantly stimulated by masturbation, fantasies, and porn.

- Sex is like a fire. Many men are constantly feeding that fire, but if it is not possible to have sex with your wife you are better off, especially as a Christian, keeping the fire burning low.

3. The easy access to porn is lethal. Things arrive uninvited in Emails, and it's not just the internet – TV, magazines...you already know the many things that grab our attention. There is little that numbs the spirit like porn.

- Porn is an addiction. You may need deliverance to get free, or a support group like Celebrate Recovery.

- Do whatever it takes to put appropriate filters on your computer.

- Destroy any porn you have, or it will destroy you.

4. Like Joseph in Egypt, flee from sexual immorality. The moment you start considering temptation and reasoning in your head, you have already lost the battle.

5. Memorize and use I Corinthians 10:13: *No temptation has overtaken you except what is common to mankind. And God is faithful; he will not let you be tempted beyond what you can bear. But when you are tempted, he will also provide a way out so that you can endure it.* It is possible to win the battle with lust.

6. Many men struggle with attraction to other men (and often feel great guilt about it). Just as any temptation is not sin unless you act on it, same sex attraction is not sin unless it is acted on or fostered in fantasies and pornography. A Christian subject to same sex attraction must remain celibate. Gay or straight, we are commanded to avoid sexual sin. Since gay marriage clearly is not

an option for anyone who accepts the truth of the Bible, the only option for someone tempted by same-sex attraction is to abstain. He is no different than a single straight male who is tempted with porn, prostitutes, or masturbation.

7. We are not blind. We are going to notice beautiful women, but keep it to one look, and give thanks to God for his beautiful creation. Train your thoughts to stop there.

Be careful of who you hang out with, and avoid those places where you know you will be tempted.

Your wife is probably not the best one to share your struggles with. Knowing her man is viewing pornography can foster insecurity and bring more problems to your sexual relationship. Find a brother to pray with and keep you accountable. We are in this battle together, and we will overcome! Sex is one of the great blessings God has given us, but if we don't follow his design, it can become a curse. My prayer is that God would set you free from sexual sin, to enjoy the woman God has given you.

1 Corinthians 7

[1] Now for the matters you wrote about: It is good for a man not to marry. [2] But since there is so much immorality, each man should have his own wife, and each woman her own husband. [3] The husband should fulfill his marital duty to his wife, and likewise the wife to her husband. [4] The wife's body does not belong to her alone but also to her husband. In the same way, the husband's body does not belong to him alone but also to his wife. [5] Do not deprive each other except by mutual consent and for a time, so that you may devote yourselves to prayer. Then come together again so that Satan will not tempt you because of your lack of self-control. [6] I say this as a concession, not as a command. [7] I wish that all men were as I am. But each man has his own gift from God; one has this gift, another has that.

[8] Now to the unmarried and the widows I say: It is good for them to stay unmarried, as I am. [9] But if they cannot control themselves, they should marry, for it is better to marry than to burn with passion.

[10] To the married I give this command (not I, but the Lord): A wife must not separate from her husband. [11] But if she does, she must remain unmarried or else be reconciled to her husband. And a husband must not divorce his wife.

[12] To the rest I say this (I, not the Lord): If any brother has a wife who is not a believer and she is willing to live with him, he must not divorce her. [13] And if a woman has a husband who is not a believer and he is willing to live with her, she must not divorce him. [14] For the unbelieving husband has been sanctified through his wife, and the unbelieving wife has been sanctified through her believing husband. Otherwise your children would be unclean, but as it is, they are holy.

[15] But if the unbeliever leaves, let him do so. A believing man or woman is not bound in such circumstances; God has called us to live in peace. [16] How do you know, wife, whether you will save your husband? Or, how do you know, husband, whether you will save your wife?

[28] *But if you do marry, you have not sinned; and if a virgin marries, she has not sinned. But those who marry will face many troubles in this life, and I want to spare you this.*

[29] *What I mean, brothers, is that the time is short. From now on those who have wives should live as if they had none;* [30] *those who mourn, as if they did not; those who are happy, as if they were not; those who buy something, as if it were not theirs to keep;* [31] *those who use the things of the world, as if not engrossed in them. For this world in its present form is passing away.*

[32] *I would like you to be free from concern. An unmarried man is concerned about the Lord's affairs—how he can please the Lord.* [33] *But a married man is concerned about the affairs of this world—how he can please his wife—* [34] *and his interests are divided. An unmarried woman or virgin is concerned about the Lord's affairs: Her aim is to be devoted to the Lord in both body and spirit. But a married woman is concerned about the affairs of this world—how she can please her husband.* [35] *I am saying this for your own good, not to restrict you, but that you may live in a right way in undivided devotion to the Lord.*

[39] *A woman is bound to her husband as long as he lives. But if her husband dies, she is free to marry anyone she wishes, but he must belong to the Lord.* [40] *In my judgment, she is happier if she stays as she is—and I think that I too have the Spirit of God.*

11

Marriage and Divorce
1 Corinthians 7

Paul wasn't a big fan of marriage, but he would have been shocked at the state of marriage in twenty first century America. This single apostle who lived 2000 years ago has a lot to teach us. This is a complicated and difficult chapter (like any marriage!), and, like so many things in this letter, it is controversial. It is never easy for men to talk about their most intimate experiences, and Paul has some clear and forceful things to say about sex, the balance of family and serving God, and divorce and remarriage.

Is it better not to marry?

The chapter starts with a strange attention-getter: *It is good for a man not to have sexual relations with a woman.* In fact, Paul is so happy with his single state he says *I wish that all of you were as I am* (7), and *it is good to stay unmarried, as I do* (8). Almost as a concession, he admits it is not a gift everyone has (and most don't want!).

What does Paul have against marriage?

- Apparently there was some crisis in Corinth, and under the circumstances Paul felt it was no time to think about marriage (26).

- He wants the believer to *be free from concern* (32), free to serve Christ and *to live in a right way in undivided devotion to the Lord* (35).

- *An unmarried man is concerned about the Lord's affairs - how he can please the Lord* (32). *An unmarried woman or virgin is concerned about the Lord's affairs: Her aim is to be devoted to the Lord in both body and spirit* (34).

- On the other hand, *the married man is concerned about the affairs of this world - how he can please his wife* (33-34). That is good, but as a result *his interests are divided*, which does affect his service for Christ, especially if he has children. *In the same way, a married woman is concerned about the affairs of this world - how she can please her husband* (34). Men like that!

- *Those who marry will face many troubles in this life* (28). I know many who would say Amen to that!

Thus some will decide to stay single and dedicate themselves to serving the Lord. Celibacy should never be required, but Paul clearly feels it is the better option, even though most of us feel it is more of a curse.

Live with the mindset that this world is passing away

Apart from the crisis in Corinth, Paul shares a principle that applies until Christ returns (29-31). There is not much time left to evangelize and prepare the church. The harvest is plentiful, but the workers are few. If that was true 2000 years ago, imagine how little time we have now! We should take this seriously!

- *Those who have wives should live as if they do not.*
- *Those who mourn, as if they did not.*
- *Those who are happy, as if they were not.*
- *Those who buy something, as if it were not theirs to keep.*
- *Those who use the things of the world, as if not engrossed in them.*

That goes way beyond marriage! It touches at the heart of the American lifestyle. It is not sinful to buy something or use the things of the world - he doesn't forbid them - but we should not get engrossed in them or hold onto them. Why? *This world in its present form is passing away.* This world is not our home. Paul wasn't saying that a married man should live as if he were single; that would contradict much of what he says in the same chapter. But our service for the Lord should have priority. There is urgency. The time is short.

And the family?

Verse 29 is very controversial, because the common teaching today is that family has priority over service for God. Certainly the New Testament is clear that someone whose family is not in order is not fit to be a leader in the church:

An elder must be blameless, faithful to his wife, a man whose children believe and are not open to the charge of being wild and disobedient (Titus 1:6).

He must manage his own family well and see that his children obey him, and he must do so in a manner worthy of full respect. (If anyone does not know how to manage his own family, how can he take care of God's church?) (1

Timothy 3:4-5).

We know that a man is to love his wife as Christ loved the church (Ephesians 5:25), and in this same letter (9:5) Paul says that the apostles traveled with their wives.

But we are not under the law, and there is no hard and fast rule that applies to every family and marriage. In some cases the family requires more attention, and in others, perhaps when there are no children, there is freedom to devote more time to the church. A couple should seek God together, and, guided by the Holy Spirit, come to agreement. From what Paul says, it is clear that a married man cannot dedicate as much time to the church as a single man. But a healthy marriage can contribute much to the overall life of the church. A happy marriage strengthens a pastor, while a troubled marriage can sap his energy and peace.

Jesus' attitude toward the family

It is interesting that Jesus never taught his disciples (from what we have recorded in the Gospels) about family responsibilities. He had no problem calling them to leave everything (family included, we could assume) to follow him and travel together. In fact, Jesus said some things that make us think twice about our focus on (and near idolatry of) the family:

Do you think I came to bring peace on earth? No, I tell you, but division. From now on there will be five in one family divided against each other, three against two and two against three. They will be divided, father against son and son against father, mother against daughter and daughter against mother, mother-in-law against daughter-in-law and daughter-in-law against mother-in-law" (Luke 12:51-53).

Peter said to him, "We have left all we had to follow you!" "Truly I tell you," Jesus said to them, "no one who has left home or wife or brothers or sisters or parents or children for the sake of the kingdom of God will fail to receive many times as much in this age, and in the age to come eternal life" (Luke 18:28-30).

"If anyone comes to me and does not hate father and mother, wife and children, brothers and sisters—yes, even their own life—such a person cannot be my disciple. And whoever does not carry their cross and follow me cannot be my disciple" (Luke 14:26-27).

As they were walking along the road, a man said to him, "I will follow you wherever you go."
Jesus replied, "Foxes have dens and birds have nests, but the Son of Man has no place to lay his head." He said to another man, "Follow me."
But he replied, "Lord, first let me go and bury my father."
Jesus said to him, "Let the dead bury their own dead, but you go and proclaim the kingdom of God."
Still another said, "I will follow you, Lord; but first let me go back and say goodbye to my family."
Jesus replied, "No one who puts a hand to the plow and looks back is fit for service in the kingdom of God" (Luke 9:57-62).

And look at what he said about his own family when they came to visit him:

Someone told him, "Your mother and brothers are standing outside, wanting to speak to you."
He replied to him, "Who is my mother, and who are my brothers?" Pointing to his disciples, he said, "Here are my mother and my brothers. For whoever does the will of my Father in heaven is my brother and sister and mother" (Matthew 12:47-50).

A perspective from the past

When we read about the family in books from many years ago, it is clear the authors were not as "illuminated" as we are about the importance of the family.

Albert Barnes was a highly regarded theologian in the US in the nineteenth century. This is the commentary he wrote about these verses in 1 Corinthians:

> This does not mean that they are to treat them with unkindness or neglect, or fail in the duties of love and fidelity. It is to be taken in a general sense, that they were to live above the world; that they were not to be unduly attached to them that they were to be ready to part with them; and that they should not suffer attachment to them to interfere with any duty which they owed to God. They were in a world of trial; and they were exposed to persecution; and as Christians they were bound to live entirely to God, and they ought not, therefore, to allow attachment to earthly friends to alienate their affections from God, or to interfere with their Christian duty. In one word, they ought to be

"just as faithful to God," and "just as pious," in every respect, as if they had no wife and no earthly friend. Such a consecration to God is difficult, but not impossible. Our earthly attachments and cares draw away our affections from God, but they need not do it. Instead of being the occasion of alienating our affections from God, they should be, and they might be, the means of binding us more firmly and entirely to him and to his cause. But alas, how many professing Christians live for their wives and children only, and not for God in these relations! How many suffer these earthly objects of attachment to alienate their minds from the ways and commandments of God, rather than make them the occasion of uniting them more tenderly to him and his cause!

By no means do I want to suggest it is fine to ignore the family. Many pastor's families have suffered because he failed to give them sufficient time, and many pastor's children have left the Lord because of their father's bad example. But the truth is that Jesus' disciples spent a good amount of time away from their families. We know, for example, that after the resurrection Peter traveled extensively.

Many have tried to make a distinction between our *relationship* to God and our *service* for God. That may be true for those called to full-time ministry, but it would seem not to apply to the service to God and others that should be part of every believer's discipleship. God, and what God requires of us, has priority over everything, including the family. I believe the two should not be in competition, but part of the sincere submission of all of life to

Christ's lordship. There is no legalistic separation, but freedom to love and serve as guided by the Holy Spirit. I know that may not satisfy many who want to justify their position (whether it the priority of the family or of Christian service), and you may see me as indecisive, but I believe every person and family should establish those priorities in God's presence. I certainly do not intend to establish a doctrine from one verse; that is dangerous. I only wish to provide some perspectives for your reflection and prayers. We must take all of Scripture seriously, allowing our pet doctrines to be molded by God's Word, and not always see the Bible through twenty-first century lenses.

Sex in marriage

Although Paul has compelling reasons not to marry, he is also a realist. He knows most of us lack self-control and will "burn" with passion. That is why God designed marriage. If we follow this counsel, we should be sexually satisfied.

- *The husband should fulfill his marital duty to his wife, and likewise the wife to her husband* (3). Sex should be frequent, and never withheld as a weapon. "Fulfilling the marital duty" is more than just dutifully making yourself available; it implies real involvement by both. But it also needs to take place in the context of the husband's Christ-like love (Ephesians 5:25). The woman should never feel violated.

- *The wife does not have authority over her own body but yields it to her husband. In the same way, the husband does not have authority over his own body but yields it to his wife* (4). Men love this verse! As one flesh, there should be a joyful intimacy and desire to give of yourself to your spouse. Unfortunately, it seems that a man is often much more willing to yield his body than his wife is!

- *Do not deprive each other* (5).

- The only exception to that would be *by mutual consent and for a time, so that you may devote yourselves to prayer* (5). Both must agree.

- If for some reason there is a time without sexual relations, *come together again* as soon as possible, so that *Satan will not tempt you because of your lack of self-control* (5). Many lack self-control, and God's solution is a vibrant sex life, which should eliminate most sexual sin. If problems persist in the sexual relationship, there may be a need for professional help.

Separation and divorce

Here is a topic so sensitive and controversial that an entire book could be (and has been) devoted to an in-depth study of the Scriptures involved. I know too many people who have agonized through heart-wrenching divorces. The last thing I want to do is add more condemnation. Yet no one benefits by ignoring Scriptures they do not agree with, and some may find encouragement and renewed faith by seeing what the Bible actually says.

Three important Old Testament teachings will help us understand what Paul is saying here:

1. God's plan for marriage was a permanent, life-long, union of one man and one woman.

- *For this reason a man shall leave his father and his mother, and be joined to his wife; and they shall become one flesh* (Genesis 2:24, NASB).
- God never made a provision for divorce: *Jesus replied, "Moses permitted divorce only as a concession to your hard hearts, but it was not what God had originally intended"* (Mathew 19:8, NLT). Obviously a Christian should not have a hard heart, or settle for second best.

2. Adultery (anything which violates that sacred union), is a very serious sin.

- It is prohibited in the Ten Commandments: *You shall not commit adultery* (Exodus 20:14).
- The penalty for adultery under the law was death: If a man commits adultery with another man's wife—with the wife of his neighbor—both the adulterer and the adulteress are to be put to death (Leviticus 20:10); *If a man is found sleeping with another man's wife, both the man who slept with her and the woman must die. You must purge the evil from Israel* (Deuteronomy 22:22).
- Adultery is self-destructive: *But the man who commits adultery is an utter fool, for he destroys himself* (Proverbs 6:32, NLT).
- One problem with divorce is that it can easily lead to adultery: *He answered, "Anyone who divorces his wife and marries another woman commits adultery against her. And if she divorces her husband and marries another man, she commits adultery"* (Mark 10:11-12).
- Paul already said (6:9) that the person who remains in adultery is not saved; will not enter the Kingdom of heaven.

3. God hates divorce: *"For I hate divorce," says the Lord, the God of Israel, "and him who covers his garment with wrong," says the Lord of hosts. "So take heed to your spirit, that you do not deal treacherously."* (Malachi 2:16, NASB).

- Paul likened the union of a man and woman to the union of Christ and his church (Ephesians 5:27 & 32).
- Jesus said: *"But at the beginning of creation God 'made them male and female.' 'For this reason a man will leave his father and mother and be united to his wife, and the two will become one flesh.' So they are no longer two, but one flesh. Therefore what God has joined together, let no one separate"* (Mark 10:6-9). No one should separate what God has united. A court decree does not change the fact that they are one flesh.

Paul's teaching flows from that understanding of Scripture:

- The Lord commands: *A wife must not separate from her husband* (10).*A woman is bound to her husband as long as he lives* (39).
- Paul affirms that again in Romans 7:2: *By law a married woman is bound to her husband as long as he is alive, but if her husband dies, she is released from the law that binds her to him.*
- *A husband must not divorce his wife* (11).
- If, despite these clear commands, separation takes place, she must *remain unmarried or else be reconciled to her husband* (11). Those are the only biblical options.

What happens when one accepts Christ and the other is not a believer? This is a special case:

- *If any brother has a wife who is not a believer and she is willing to live with him, he must not divorce her* (12). The same is true if the husband is an unbeliever (13).*If the unbeliever leaves, let it be so. The brother or the sister is not bound in such circumstances* (15). Note that Paul says "leaves," and not "divorces."

- *God has called us to live in peace* (15). The idea is that the unbeliever might be abusive or resist staying with a believer. Some have mistakenly used this verse to rationalize divorce from a Christian.

- We don't fully understand it, but something happens in the spiritual realm when an unbeliever is married to a believer. *The unbelieving husband has been sanctified through his wife, and the unbelieving wife has been sanctified through her believing husband.* This seems to particularly impact children. Unless the unbelieving spouse is sanctified by the believer, the children would be unclean. The believer's presence makes them holy (14). This could not mean they are saved, but the presence of the believer in the intimacy of a family has a sanctifying influence on the whole home.

What about remarriage?

- If her husband dies, she is *free to marry anyone she wishes* (39). Presumably this would apply to a man who is widowed as well. However, Paul still thinks they would be happier if they didn't marry (40). Paul states the same in Romans: *For example, by law a married woman is bound to her husband as long as he is alive, but if her husband dies, she is released from the law that binds her to him. So then, if she has sexual relations with another man while her husband is still alive, she is called an adulteress. But if her husband dies, she is released from that law and is not an adulteress if she marries another man* (Romans 7:2-3).

- *He must belong to the Lord* (39). Both Testaments clearly teach that a believer can only marry another believer. Despite that, Christians still get involved with unbelievers - and usually pay dearly for it. Don't even consider a relationship with someone who doesn't belong to the Lord.

It comes as a surprise to many, but this is the only situation where the Bible explicitly permits remarriage. Many have believed that verse 15, where an unbeliever leaves the spouse, permits the believer to remarry. But Paul never says that; he simply says the believer is *"not bound,"* or *"not under bondage"* to make an effort to maintain the marriage. That is not the same as saying they are free to remarry. Once again, this is a gray area, and I don't intend to be dogmatic about it. But with something so serious, where my salvation is at stake, I would rather be sure than be sorry.

Scholars from the past were much less likely to allow remarriage. Albert Barnes (whom I cited previously) wrote:

"A brother or a sister is not under bondage..." Many have supposed that this means that they would be at liberty to marry again when the unbelieving wife or husband had gone away; but this is contrary to the strain of the argument of the apostle. The sense of the expression "is not bound," is that if they forcibly depart, the one that is left is not bound by the marriage tie to make provision for the one that departed; to do acts that might be prejudicial to religion by a violent effort to compel the departing husband or wife to live with the one that is

forsaken; but is at liberty to live separate, and should regard it as proper so to do.

The *Expositor's Greek New Testament* on verse 15:

Whether the freedom of the innocent divorced extends to *remarriage*, does not appear: the Roman Church takes the negative view...in view of 1 Corinthians 7:1, the inference that the divorced should remain unmarried is the safer.

And a theologian named Woodford wrote in 1881:

The separation here spoken of is not a separation allowing the Christian man or woman to marry again during the lifetime of the heathen spouse. It is separation, not divorce.

The "exception clause" in Matthew

Many Christians, based on two passages in Matthew, believe that Jesus offered an "exception" which also allowed for divorce and remarriage:

> But I tell you that anyone who divorces his wife, except for sexual immorality, makes her the victim of adultery, and anyone who marries a divorced woman commits adultery (Matthew 5:32).

> I tell you that anyone who divorces his wife, except for sexual immorality, and marries

another woman commits adultery (Matthew 19:9).

The argument is that Jesus appears to allow remarriage in the case of "sexual immorality." The problem is that he does not explicitly say that it is permitted. And the bigger problem is: What does Jesus mean by "immorality," traditionally translated "fornication." It is not the Greek word for adultery, but the Greek word *"porneia,"* which refers to any sexual sin, and is obviously the root of our word "pornography." Jesus obviously did not mean that divorce is permitted from a spouse who masturbates or uses pornography. Some believe that this "exception" is for an engaged couple (such as Joseph and Mary); at that time the engagement was ended by divorce. Both Mark and Luke, in the parallel verse, use the word for adultery, and do not include the "exception." Even in the case of adultery, God's will is always for repentance, forgiveness, and restauration.

Given that Jesus speaks so forcibly about the possibility of adultery in a second marriage, and the adulterer (unless they repent and leave the adulterous relationship) cannot enter the Kingdom, I would rather be sure, and not take a chance with something so serious. Traditionally neither the Catholic or Protestant church has believed that these verses allow remarriage. There are many books, and many studies on the internet, with various points of view. I encourage you to pray much and study the Word with an open heart to discern the truth.

The implications

This chapter opens the door to a multitude of questions, fears, doubts, and guilt:

- "I divorced and remarried. Should I divorce my current spouse and return to the first one? What if she has married someone else? Or should I just divorce and remain single?"
- "My wife is a Christian – but she left me for another man. Do you mean I can never get married again?"
- "My husband is abusive. Does God want me to continue suffering this abuse?"
- "Can I be forgiven for my adultery and divorce?" (Of course! Especially if it occurred before you knew Jesus. It is not the unforgivable sin.)

It is impossible to address all the possibilities. I know this topic is very painful and difficult, but it helps no one to pretend that the Bible doesn't clearly say what it does. I fear for the many pastors who don't want to offend anyone and don't preach the Word of God! And even more for those pastors who have divorced their wives and married another woman in the church!

God loves you! He has a way out of any situation. There is forgiveness. There is hope. Only the Holy Spirit can counsel you on what to do in every situation. Seek the Lord.

Other themes in this chapter

Paul touches on two other (less controversial) matters in this chapter:

- *Each person should live as a believer in whatever situation the Lord has assigned to them, just as God has called them* (17). Whether married, circumcised, or a slave, they should stay there until God changes it. It is a principle that can be applied to a variety of situations we encounter after salvation (17-24).

- He gives advice to those who are engaged and unsure if they should get married (25-28, 36-38).

Paul does not mention gay marriage, which was unthinkable until recently. The Bible strongly condemns homosexual relations, and doesn't even contemplate the marriage of two men or two women (Leviticus 20:13; Romans 1:24-27).

12

Food Sacrificed to Idols
- What it means for you
1 Corinthians 8

It might seem like this chapter has nothing to do with twenty first century Christianity. Who do you know that sacrifices food to an idol? But, as with all of Scripture, there is some rich teaching for us.

The Importance of Love

¹Now about food sacrificed to idols: We know that we all possess knowledge. Knowledge puffs up, but love builds up. ² The man who thinks he knows something does not yet know as he ought to know. ³ But the man who loves God is known by God.

Many Corinthians knew that nothing happens to food sacrificed to an idol; Christians are free to eat it. But not *everyone* knew that, and the "more knowledgeable" were causing them to stumble by resolutely exercising their freedom. They were sinning because they were not acting in love.

Have you ever met someone who knows everything? The typical teen who knows more than his parents? The Bible teacher who thinks he can explain everything in the Bible? The atheist who believes he can disprove everything in it?

There is nothing wrong with going to Bible school or seminary, but be careful: *Knowledge puffs up* (1). Most of Jesus' opposition came from highly educated Pharisees and teachers of the law. Those who know a lot will be tempted by pride, and need to make a conscious effort to stay humble. Jesus pointed to children as the greatest in the kingdom. In my twenties I thought I knew a lot, but with each passing year I feel I know less. Paul, a very intelligent, well-educated man, was inspired by the Spirit to write: *The man who thinks he knows something does not yet know as he ought to know* (2). The New Living Translation says: *Anyone who claims to know all the answers doesn't really know very much.*

Love is more important than knowledge! *Love builds up* (1). The first and greatest commandment is to love God. *The man who loves God is known by God* (3). God already knows everything. He is not impressed by your knowledge or displays of it. He is impressed by your love. As Paul writes later in chapter thirteen, knowledge will pass away, and at that time we will know fully. Faith, hope, and love remain, and the greatest is love.

The Nature of Idols

4 So then, about eating food sacrificed to idols: We know that an idol is nothing at all in the world and that there is no God but one. 5 For even if there are so-called gods, whether in heaven or on earth (as indeed there are many "gods" and many "lords"), 6 yet for us there is but one God, the Father, from whom all things came and for whom we live; and there is but one Lord, Jesus Christ, through whom all things came and through whom we live.

The idols common at that time are rare today, but we have plenty of our own gods, which of course aren't gods at all. God is not in competition with idols!

In saying that, Paul makes an interesting affirmation of Jesus' divinity. Though Father and Son have different titles and functions, they are both the source and purpose of all life:

There is but one God, the Father, from whom all things came and for whom we live.

There is but one Lord, Jesus Christ, through whom all things came and through whom we live. (6)

Jesus gives us a reason to live, for his Father. The two are equally God, and, along with the Holy Spirit, work together.

Freedom

[7] But not everyone knows this. Some people are still so accustomed to idols that when they eat such food they think of it as having been sacrificed to an idol, and since their conscience is weak, it is defiled. [8] But food does not bring us near to God; we are no worse if we do not eat, and no better if we do.
[9] Be careful, however, that the exercise of your freedom does not become a stumbling block to the weak. [10] For if anyone with a weak conscience sees you who have this knowledge eating in an idol's temple, won't he be emboldened to eat what has been sacrificed to idols? [11] So this weak brother, for whom Christ died, is destroyed by your knowledge. [12] When you sin against your brothers in this way and wound their weak conscience, you sin against Christ. [13] Therefore, if what I eat causes my brother to fall

into sin, I will never eat meat again, so that I will not cause him to fall.

This is a passage very similar to Romans 14. Food sacrificed to idols is one of many "gray" areas in the Christian life - things not specifically commanded or condemned by the Bible. They don't bring you closer to God or push you away from him. You are no better, more mature, or stronger if you indulge than if you choose not to. If you abstain, it doesn't make you less of a Christian, somehow implying you are weak or ignorant (8). On the other hand, those who are more conservative can fall into pride, feeling they are better Christians than the more "liberal" brother. That is not based in love, and is also sin. In everything, our first priority must be to love and edify our brothers and sisters.

What about a person brought up in a very conservative home, or in a home with many idols? In his heart he believes something is sin, but seeing an older Christian doing it, he does it. He ends up being *destroyed by your knowledge* (11). Our *freedom can become a stumbling block to the weak* (9). The person who knows more and has been a believer longer has the responsibility to love and care for the younger brother. If he insists on exercising his freedom, he sins. In love, we accommodate the other brother, so as not to *wound their weak conscience* (12). If it *causes your brother to fall into sin*, never do it again (13).

My approach on the "gray" areas has always been to err on the safe side. If there is any question, why risk it? Better to be sure than sorry.

- Are there "gray" areas you're struggling with?
- Have you become "puffed up" by your knowledge?

- Do you condemn those with a broader understanding of what is allowed for a Christian?
- Are there any areas in which you are causing someone to stumble?

May God give you wisdom and help you always make love and the building up of your brother a priority!

13

Three Strikes against Paul - But He's not out!

1 Corinthians 9

¹Am I not free? Am I not an apostle? Have I not seen Jesus our Lord? Are you not the result of my work in the Lord? ²Even though I may not be an apostle to others, surely I am to you! For you are the seal of my apostleship in the Lord.

³ This is my defense to those who sit in judgment on me. ⁴Don't we have the right to food and drink? ⁵Don't we have the right to take a believing wife along with us, as do the other apostles and the Lord's brothers and Cephas? ⁶Or is it only I and Barnabas who must work for a living?

Paul ends the chapter talking about sports. I don't know if he knew "three strikes and you're out" back then, but when it came to him being an apostle, he had three strikes against him:

- Since he had persecuted the church and wasn't one of the Twelve (he met Jesus after his ascension, on the road to Damascus), many never acknowledged him as an apostle (2).
- Many sat in judgment of him (3).

- He wasn't given the same privileges other apostles enjoyed (4-6).

It is obvious from what we have studied so far that being a Christian is not easy, and it is even harder for leaders in the church. Today we recognize Paul as a great apostle, but it wasn't always the case. He was a tough guy, but rejection by a church he had invested so much in hurt deeply. They were the seal of his apostleship (2) and the fruit of his labors (1). Somehow he must re-establish his standing with them.

The competition among apostles that so troubled Paul is probably worse today. There are some highly visible and influential pastors, while others with small churches and little education struggle to defend their calling. Like Paul and Barnabas, many of them are "tent makers," working full time while they pastor (6). Maybe you have invested your time and energy in a church, or pastor a small church. You have labored for years and had some fruit, but no one seems to recognize it. Don't worry. Paul could identify with you. Your labor in the Lord is never in vain.

A Christian worker should be paid for his labor

⁷ Who serves as a soldier at his own expense? Who plants a vineyard and does not eat of its grapes? Who tends a flock and does not drink of the milk? ⁸ Do I say this merely from a human point of view? Doesn't the Law say the same thing? ⁹ For it is written in the Law of Moses: "Do not muzzle an ox while it is treading out the grain." Is it about oxen that God is concerned? ¹⁰ Surely he says this for us, doesn't he? Yes, this was written for us, because when the plowman plows and the thresher threshes, they ought to do so in the hope of sharing in the harvest. ¹¹ If we have sown spiritual seed among you, is it too much if we reap a material harvest from you? ¹² If others have this right of support from you, shouldn't we have it all the more?

But we did not use this right. On the contrary, we put up with anything rather than hinder the gospel of Christ. ¹³ Don't you know that those who work in the temple get their food from the temple, and those who serve at the altar share in what is offered on the altar? ¹⁴ In the same way, the Lord has commanded that those who preach the gospel should receive their living from the gospel.

¹⁵ But I have not used any of these rights. And I am not writing this in the hope that you will do such things for me. I would rather die than have anyone deprive me of this boast. ¹⁶ Yet when I preach the gospel, I cannot boast, for I am compelled to preach. Woe to me if I do not preach the gospel! ¹⁷ If I preach voluntarily, I have a reward; if not voluntarily, I am simply discharging the trust committed to me. ¹⁸ What then is my reward? Just this: that in preaching the gospel I may offer it free of charge, and so not make use of my rights in preaching it.

Money has always been a sensitive issue. Knowing that, Paul builds a careful case for his right to support, starting with three examples from daily life (7):

- A soldier doesn't have to pay his own expenses.
- If you plant a vineyard you expect to eat the grapes.
- If you tend a flock, you can drink the milk it produces.

Whoever plows and threshes anticipates sharing in the harvest

(10), as commanded in the law: *"Do not muzzle an ox while it is treading out the grain"* (Deuteronomy 25:4).

- *Those who serve in the temple get their food from the temple* (13).
- *Those who serve at the altar share in what is offered on the altar* (13).
- *The Lord has commanded that those who preach the gospel should receive their living from the gospel* (14, Matthew 10:10).

Case closed. It is not sinful to be motivated by hopes of a good harvest, and it is not a sin to reap a material harvest from spiritual seed you have sown (11). Apparently the Corinthian church was supporting others, but not Paul, who had more claim to it (12)!

Having demonstrated his right to financial support, Paul turns around and shows how righteous he is by refusing it (12): *I would rather die than allow anyone to deprive me of this boast* (15). Paul was proud of not taking their money (16); it was something a little odd about his character that showed up several times. But more important than the money or his pride, he is willing to *put up with anything rather than hinder the gospel of Christ* (12). Paul didn't preach for financial gain, but out of obedience to his calling (17). I wish more leaders had that attitude today! The emphasis on money is a stumbling block for many in embracing the gospel. It would be great if we, like Paul, could present the gospel with no strings attached.

Should the church adequately pay their ministers? Yes! Should ministers be careful not to abuse money or make it a central focus? Absolutely! It is good for a church to give generously, but there may be times when it is better for the minister to refuse money.

Humble, incarnate, ministry

19 Though I am free and belong to no man, I make myself a slave to everyone, to win as many as possible. 20 To the Jews I became like a Jew, to win the Jews. To those under the law I became like one under the law (though I myself am not under the law), so as to win those under the law. 21 To those not having the law I became like one not having the law (though I am not free from God's law but am under Christ's law), so as to win those not having the law. 22 To the weak I became weak, to win the weak. I have become all things to all men so that by all possible means I might save some. 23 I do all this for the sake of the gospel, that I may share in its blessings.

Jesus' model of ministry was the incarnation: complete identification with us to the extreme of taking on our flesh. He became a humble servant. *Your attitude should be the same* (Philippians 2:5-8). We are free in Christ, but out of love we become slaves to everyone, to win as many as possible (19). Enough of lazy, self-centered pastors who are bothered by the needs of their flock! The warnings of Ezekiel 34 could be applied to many pastors! We are called to do everything possible and necessary to draw someone to the Lord.

- To the Jews, Paul was a Jew. *To those under the law I became like one under the law (though I myself am not under the law), so as to win those under the law* (20). Obviously, that wasn't hard for an ex-Pharisee like Paul, yet he chose to obey some laws he wasn't obligated to so his message would be heard.

- Among gentiles, he became like a gentile (21).
- To the weak he became weak (22).
- He became all things to all men (22). *Yes, I try to find common ground with everyone, doing everything I can to save some* (NLT).

To some extent, the ends justify the means. We do whatever it takes, as long as we maintain our integrity, so that by all possible means some might be saved (22). Not so we can be famous, but for the sake of the gospel. There was nothing patronizing or false in what Paul did. He was free to do this because he was secure in his own identity. Without compromising your faith, do whatever you can to identify with other people, possibly adopting their way of life, their food, their clothing, and their language. That means we make it our business to study the people we are trying to reach, so we can become like them.

Is that your model of ministry?

- Do you need to humble yourself and leave your comfort zone to enter into another culture?
- Have you over-identified with the culture around you?
- What about your church? Is it so far removed from the surrounding culture that it's irrelevant? Or so closely identified with the culture that it's no different than the world?

Let the Spirit lead you to the right balance, and remember the purpose is to win them to Christ. In doing so, don't water down the gospel. Paul certainly didn't.

Go for the prize!

[24] Do you not know that in a race all the runners run, but only one gets the prize? Run in such a way as to get the prize.[25] Everyone who competes in the games goes into strict training. They do it to get a crown that will not last, but we do it to get a crown that will last forever. [26] Therefore I do not run like someone running aimlessly; I do not fight like a boxer beating the air. [27] No, I strike a blow to my body and make it my slave so that after I have preached to others, I myself will not be disqualified for the prize.

Paul ends the chapter with a challenge to every believer - and especially every leader.

- *In a race all the runners run, but only one gets the prize.* The good news in the Christian race is we can all get the prize!
- Athletes go into strict training to get a crown that won't last (24-25).

What does that mean for you?

- *Run in such a way as to get the prize* (24). Total focus and dedication, with your eyes on the prize. To get a crown that will last forever you must discipline and train yourself.
- Run with purpose, not aimlessly (26).
- Know who you are fighting, not like someone beating the air.
- Beat your body and make it your slave (27).
- Make sure at the end of the day you are not disqualified for the prize. Even Paul was aware of that possibility (27).

That is a strong challenge? How are you doing in the race?

- Are you tired?
- Discouraged?
- Does that prize seem out of reach?
- Are you ready to give up?
- Are you wandering around aimlessly?
- Wasting your time and energy?
- Have you lost your sense of purpose?
- Is it time to seek God and evaluate what you are doing?
- Are you beating the air, while the real enemy is beating you up?
- Are you beating your body, or are you its slave, jumping at its every desire for food, rest, and pleasure?

Get up and fight with a purpose! Get back in the race!

- Get back in the ring!
- Beat your body!
- Don't give up!
- Make sure you're not disqualified!
- If you can barely move because you have been ignoring your need for rest and nourishment, take some time to regain your balance.

We used to live next to the Verrazano Narrows Bridge in Brooklyn. Thousands of people would flood over that bridge at the start of the New York Marathon, but a relative trickle would finish. Many start strong in this race, but what really matters is how we finish. We need endurance. Unfortunately, many are disqualified. I don't want you to be among them.

A final note: Apostles today

There is a lot of talk today about apostles. Fifty years ago practically no one would claim to be an apostle; today it seems like everyone is! Paul's letters teach us a lot about apostles. In this chapter we have seen:

- The seal of apostleship is a church you've established and supervise (2).
- A church should ensure an apostle has adequate food, drink, and other necessities (4).
- He has a right to support from the church he founded (11-12). An apostle should not be forced to work for a living (6).
- An apostle usually travels, and has the right for his wife to accompany him (5).
- Jesus' brothers traveled, were married, and were included among the apostles.
- In the New Testament apostles were always men. Most of them seem to be married with a believing wife.

As we study Paul's life and writings, we are reminded that it is not easy to serve the Lord, and it is probably hardest for an apostle!

14

How not to be Disqualified from the Race

1 Corinthians 10:1-13

Unfortunately, the artificial divisions in our Bibles interrupt the flow of Paul's thought. To understand this chapter we must look back to the end of the previous chapter:

- We are in a race that requires self-control if we are to win the prize.
- Even someone who has preached and ministered to others can be disqualified.

An example of being disqualified and losing the race

[1]For I do not want you to be ignorant of the fact, brothers, that our forefathers were all under the cloud and that they all passed through the sea. [2] They were all baptized into Moses in the cloud and in the sea. [3] They all ate the same spiritual food [4] and drank the same spiritual drink; for they drank from the spiritual rock that accompanied them, and that rock was Christ.

The majority of the Israelites were disqualified despite amazing experiences with God (1-4):

- They were all guided and protected by the cloud and pillar of fire when they left Egypt.
- They all miraculously passed through the Red Sea (see Exodus 14).
- In the cloud and sea they were baptized into Moses, who is a type of Jesus. Under Moses' leadership, the entire nation moved from slavery into God's plan of redemption, foreshadowing our baptism into God's plan of salvation under Christ's Lordship.
- They all ate the same spiritual food - both manna, and the word Moses received from God.
- They all drank the same spiritual drink - water that miraculously came from the rock.

Now Paul introduces a new concept: it wasn't just water. The rock that gave them life-giving water on their journey was Christ. Jesus himself was with them on the Exodus, possibly as the "angel of the Lord" we read about. The spiritual food and drink foreshadowed the Lord's Supper.

What more could you ask for?

They had all these benefits: God's presence and miraculous provision.

⁵Nevertheless, God was not pleased with most of them; their bodies were scattered in the wilderness.

They never entered the promised land. They died. God was not pleased with them. Paul has warned the Corinthians that God is not pleased with them, either. They may be baptized and partake in the Lord's Supper, but if they continue in their sin, they will perish. How could Israel lose it all when God had done so much for them? How can we be disqualified, having the Scriptures, knowing Jesus, and tasting of the Holy Spirit?

[6] Now these things occurred as examples to keep us from setting our hearts on (craving, coveting, lusting after, Amplified Bible) *evil things as they did.*

We not only have Israel, but also the example of godly believers through the centuries. There are four important things to avoid:

Idolatry: *[7]Do not be idolaters, as some of them were; as it is written: "The people sat down to eat and drink and got up to indulge in revelry."* Here Paul is talking about the golden calf (see Exodus 32), although Israel continually fell into idolatry. Their eating, drinking, and revelry remind me of our world today.

Sexual sin: *[8]We should not commit sexual immorality, as some of them did—and in one day twenty-three thousand of them died.* In Numbers 25 the Israelites indulged in sex with Moabite women. God wanted to destroy the whole nation, but Aaron's grandson Phinehas drove a spear through an Israeli man who was laying with a Moabite woman, and stopped the plague. I am not encouraging you to search out couples in sin to spear them, but how can we stop the plague of sexual sin in the church? How many would die if God brought the same judgment on us?

Putting the Lord to the test: *[9]We should not test Christ, as some of them did—and were killed by snakes.* How do we put the Lord to the test? Israel murmured against him, not trusting him to provide when there was no water (Exodus 17). In Numbers 21 they grew impatient, detesting the "miserable food" (manna and quail) God had given them, and speaking against God and Moses. They wanted to see how far they could go, just as many Christians try to see how much they can sin and still keep their salvation. We test the Lord when we question him, his plan, and his provision.

Grumbling against God: *¹⁰And do not grumble, as some of them did —and were killed by the destroying angel.* They grumbled when there was no food or water, and when God judged them after Korah's rebellion (Numbers 16). God commands us to be thankful in everything. It is very easy to fall into grumbling and complaining.

In each case the punishment was death - and the Corinthians had already committed these sins! No wonder Paul was concerned for their salvation! Don't repeat past mistakes - your own, your parents', or Israel's.

¹¹ These things happened to them as examples and were written down as warnings for us, on whom the fulfillment of the ages has come.

Pay attention to these warnings! We have a special responsibility; during this time of grace and salvation in Christ, we are experiencing the *"fulfillment of the ages."* What a blessing to have the privilege of living in the end times!

The danger of self-confidence

The Corinthians thought they were doing great. Many Christians believe they are standing firm, but self-confidence is dangerous:

¹²If you think you are standing firm, be careful that you don't fall!

Maybe Paul was thinking about the race again. The devil is prowling around, looking for someone to trip up. Watch out for him! No one is exempt from sin, but God is for you and with you in the time of temptation.

A way out of temptation

¹³No temptation has overtaken you except what is common to mankind. And God is faithful; he will not let you be tempted beyond what you can bear. But when you are tempted, he will also provide a way out so that you can endure it.

- We all experience temptation. You have not experienced any temptation that others have not battled. The devil will say your temptation is unique, or tougher to resist, but that is a lie.

- God is faithful. Trust him! He loves you! He will help you! Call out to him!

- He will not allow you to be tempted beyond what you can bear (or resist). He knows how strong you are. If you have little temptation, maybe your faith is weak. Or it could mean that you have already resisted and overcome much temptation. If the temptation is strong, it could be that God knows you are able to bear a lot. God is sovereign, and you will only be tempted by what he allows.

- When (it doesn't say *if*, but *when*) you are tempted, God will give you a way out so you can stand up under it (or resist it). But you must *want* to get out. You have to resist and run from the temptation. The truth is many times we don't want to escape the temptation. We want to fall into it - and then ask forgiveness later. Be careful; you are playing with God.

Learn from Israel's example! Don't fall into the same sins! Fight temptation and ask God to show you the way out. He wants you to win the prize! He is faithful and will always provide the way - if you want to take it.

15

The Lord's Supper
1 Corinthians 10:14-22 and 11:17-34

In my childhood church you couldn't take communion before confirmation - around thirteen. I was jealous of my parents - it seemed so mystical, opening a new dimension of intimacy with Jesus. Finally the day arrived for my first communion. I had high expectations, and...nothing! That disappointment was the first step toward my leaving the church and the Lord.

Unfortunately, many Christians find communion disappointing. They take the Lord's Supper because everyone else does. You are supposed to. Some churches routinely do it on the first Sunday of the month; some only a few times a year. Often even the pastor doesn't seem too excited, rushing through it at the end of the service, when everyone is anxious to get home. Some churches at least surround the supper with meaningful liturgy, although many who were raised in those churches have reacted against the ritual. Many evangelical churches hardly say anything about it. I have been in churches where you can walk to the back and help yourself if you want communion. Former Catholics reject the near idolatry of the mass and the belief that the wine actually becomes Jesus' blood and the bread becomes his body. We believe they are symbols - what you are taking is grape juice and bread. But in our emphasis on the symbolic, we forget that Christians through the centuries have believed the supper to be a "means of grace." Since Jesus commanded us to observe it, he is present in it, and we can expect to experience a special grace as we partake.

In the first part of 1 Corinthians 10, Paul used Israel's example as a warning not to be disqualified in the race and lose our prize. One of their sins was idolatry, and he starts his teaching on the Lord's Supper (verse 14) with another warning: *14 Therefore, my dear friends, flee from idolatry.* The idol worship of the day often included common meals and offering the idol food and drink.

The problem with idolatry

19 Do I mean then that food sacrificed to an idol is anything, or that an idol is anything? 20 No, but the sacrifices of pagans are offered to demons, not to God, and I do not want you to be participants with demons.

Nothing happens to food sacrificed to an idol, which is just a piece of wood or metal (as Paul already had stated in 8:4-6). But behind every idol, every false religion, and those who take part in their ceremonies, are demons. There is a real possibility of being demonized, since they actually have "communion" with those demons.

21 You cannot drink the cup of the Lord and the cup of demons too; you cannot have a part in both the Lord's table and the table of demons. 22 Are we trying to arouse the Lord's jealousy? Are we stronger than he?

Apparently some believers were still involved in idolatry. But God is a jealous god, and it is almost blasphemous to drink both the cup of the Lord and the cup of demons. That may seem irrelevant today, but we don't want to give up our "idols" either. Aren't there other ways we take part in things that are demonic? In our entertainment, for example? You can't be double-minded and serve two masters. You have to choose one and reject the other.

18 Consider the people of Israel: Do not those who eat the sacrifices participate in the altar?

Jews understood the meaning of sacrifices. The person making the sacrifice would enter into communion both with God, who received the sacrifice on the altar, and with others who were eating the sacrificed meat.

What we learn about the Supper in chapter 10

16 Is not the cup of thanksgiving for which we give thanks a participation in the blood of Christ? And is not the bread that we break a participation in the body of Christ?

The Greek word translated "communion" or "participation" is *koinonia*. For the Christian, it speaks of fellowship with the Lord and other believers. We are one in and with Christ, and the Supper is the ultimate expression of that fellowship. The Bible often speaks of our union with Christ and him living in us. We actually eat and drink these symbols of Jesus' life (bread and wine). They become part of us, filling us and giving us spiritual nourishment. We should leave the table strengthened.

The bread not only symbolizes Christ's physical body; Paul relates it to our communion with other believers: *17 Because there is one loaf, we, who are many, are one body, for we all share the one loaf*. We take the Supper as individuals, but it also celebrates our unity, a theme Paul will develop in chapter twelve. By its very nature, communion should be a corporate experience. There is important symbolism in a single loaf, from which we each take a piece. It may be more appropriate than the cardboard-like wafers many churches use!

Paul addresses other problems with the Supper in the second part of chapter eleven

[18] In the first place, I hear that when you come together as a church, there are divisions among you, and to some extent I believe it. [19] No doubt there have to be differences among you to show which of you have God's approval.

Instead of demonstrating unity, their observance of the Supper magnified the divisions Paul addressed earlier in the letter, with various groups striving to show who was best.

[20] So then, when you come together, it is not the Lord's Supper you eat, [21] for when you are eating, some of you go ahead with your own private suppers. As a result, one person remains hungry and another gets drunk. [22] Don't you have homes to eat and drink in? Or do you despise the church of God by humiliating those who have nothing? What shall I say to you? Shall I praise you? Certainly not in this matter!

[33] So then, my brothers and sisters, when you gather to eat, you should all eat together. [34] Anyone who is hungry should eat something at home, so that when you meet together it may not result in judgment.

Paul is referring to the love feasts common in the early church, not unlike our potluck dinners. There is nothing wrong with having a meal along with communion, but some - particularly the poor – were not allowed to eat the best food. The wealthy and most popular ate first, and some ended up leaving hungry. Wine flowed freely, and many got drunk. They were missing the meaning of the Supper, and lacking reverence for Christ's presence. In this situation Paul says it would be better to eat at home. These abuses may seem foreign to us, but we too fail to understand the importance of communion. There needs to be order in our observance of the Supper.

How to celebrate the Supper

23 For I received from the Lord what I also passed on to you: The Lord Jesus, on the night he was betrayed, took bread, 24 and when he had given thanks, he broke it and said, "This is my body, which is for you; do this in remembrance of me."

The command and instructions on how to celebrate the Supper came directly from Jesus. This intimate Supper was the highlight of his last night with the disciples in the upper room, the night he was betrayed. We must do everything necessary to make sure it is taken seriously and never becomes an empty, pious, ritual. The whole focus is on Jesus. It is appropriate to read from the Gospels, sing some worship songs about Jesus' saving work, and have an open time of prayer. The Supper points us to the central tenets of our faith: Jesus' life, his sacrificial death on the cross, and his victorious resurrection. We need to be reminded of that, especially when it is rare to hear about sin, repentance, and a true relationship with Jesus. Today's church seems to be more focused on living a happy, successful life, and how God will help you do that.

²⁵In the same way, after supper he took the cup, saying, "This cup is the new covenant in my blood; do this, whenever you drink it, in remembrance of me."

The supper initiated the New Covenant. Covenants were usually sealed with blood - in this case the blood of Jesus. Each time we take the cup we give thanks for Jesus' faithfulness to that covenant, and reaffirm our commitment to it.

²⁶For whenever you eat this bread and drink this cup, you proclaim the Lord's death until he comes.

In the Supper we release the power of Jesus' shed blood as we proclaim his death to demons, principalities and powers, and the world. Looking back to the cross and forward to the Wedding of the Lamb, we will continue celebrating the Supper until Jesus returns (Matthew 26:29).

²⁷So then, whoever eats the bread or drinks the cup of the Lord in an unworthy manner will be guilty of sinning against the body and blood of the Lord.

From what we have seen so far, the importance of the Supper should be obvious. To be guilty of sinning against Jesus' blood and body is very serious. Partaking of the Supper in an unworthy manner makes us guilty, whether it is the abuses Paul has described, or anything else which devalues it. Whoever officiates at the Supper is responsible to ensure it is taken properly. New believers must be given proper orientation. In the past, church leadership appreciated its importance and restricted it to those whom they knew understood what it meant. Though there is joy and thanksgiving as we approach the table, there should also be reverence and even fear.

[28]Everyone ought to examine themselves before they eat of the bread and drink from the cup.

[31]But if we were more discerning with regard to ourselves, we would not come under such judgment. [32]Nevertheless, when we are judged in this way by the Lord, we are being disciplined so that we will not be finally condemned with the world.

A very important - and often overlooked - part of the Supper is self-examination. Is there someone we need to forgive (see Matthew 5:23-24)? Is there sin we need to confess? Is repentance needed? Even though it is uncomfortable, when we truly open ourselves to the Holy Spirit and the Lord's discipline, God can move in our lives. If we don't, Paul warns, we may be condemned along with the world.

[29]For those who eat and drink without discerning the body of Christ eat and drink judgment on themselves. [30]That is why many among you are weak and sick, and a number of you have fallen asleep.

We can actually bring condemnation, or judgment, on ourselves if we take the Supper incorrectly. It is the leader's responsibility to help the church "discern the body." What does that mean? Some believe the "body" is the church (the body of Christ), since Paul already talked about the Corinthians' problem with unity and their practice of the Supper, and in chapter 12 will write more about the church. Or it could mean taking the Supper without discerning the meaning of Jesus' crucified body. The Supper is so important and powerful that partaking incorrectly can result in weakness, sickness, and even death. So much for those who insist it is merely symbolic!

Some read these verses and, feeling unworthy or fearful, don't want to partake. But no one is worthy, and to not take the Supper is to disobey Christ's command! Instead, encourage the congregation to examine themselves, accept Christ if they haven't, repent if they need to, and get right with God so they can joyfully and thankfully receive communion.

As we conclude the Supper it is good to minister to individuals in prayer, give an opportunity for everyone to pray in petition or thanksgiving, and worship the Lord in song. Jesus is very present at that moment, and we can expect healing, deliverance, or other ministry to take place.

Don't you think Jesus deserves the best for his Supper? Each part should be directed by the Spirit, not just done by rote. We should carefully and prayerfully prepare for each observance, expecting a supernatural encounter with Jesus. If we don't, we are in great danger of taking the Supper in an "unworthy manner." I pray that you would find Jesus' Supper an increasingly meaningful time of communion with him and his church.

16

Eight Guidelines to Help in Decision Making
1 Corinthians 10:23-11:1

Many things in the Bible (the Ten Commandments, for example), are black and white. But there are other "gray areas" where there is no specific biblical counsel - things that may not even have existed in biblical times. Here Paul summarizes what he has covered in the previous chapters, and gives us simple yet profound principles to evaluate every decision you face.

23"I have the right to do anything," you say—but not everything is beneficial. "I have the right to do anything"—but not everything is constructive.

1. **Is it helpful? Does it benefit me - and others?** We are not under the law, but we need to use our freedom wisely. Many movies, games, and television programs are of no benefit to me, and I avoid them. But be careful of a pharisaical legalism - allow others the freedom to make their own decisions.

2. **Is it constructive? Does it help me grow spiritually? Does it edify?** Many years ago I worked as a DJ at a radio station. I love music, but lots of music draws me away from the Lord instead of

closer to him. It may be permitted, but I choose not to listen to it. Many things on the internet don't edify. What is good is often the enemy of the best. Life is short. I want to devote my life to constructive, edifying, things.

[24] No one should seek their own good, but the good of others.

3. Am I looking out for others' interests? Or just my own? We tend to be selfish. If we take this principle seriously, I suspect we will spend much more time and energy helping others. At home, when you decide how to spend an afternoon, do you look out for the interests of your wife and children, or just your own? At work, on the road, and with your money, do you look out for others' interests? There is a healthy balance of taking care of yourself while looking out for the interests of others.

[25] Eat anything sold in the meat market without raising questions of conscience, [26] for, "The earth is the Lord's, and everything in it."

4. Am I using what God has given me wisely, in the way he designed it to be used? All God's creation is good and was made for our enjoyment: *Everything God created is good, and nothing is to be rejected if it is received with thanksgiving* (1 Timothy 4:4), but that doesn't mean we can go crazy with it. We need to exercise wisdom and enjoy it according to its purpose. For example, we enjoy sex, but in the context of marriage, as we believe God intended. Or food and drink. If you eat too much, and eat junk food, your health will suffer.

[31] So whether you eat or drink or whatever you do, do it all for the glory of God.

5. Is what I'm doing glorifying God? How about that joke? Your conversations? Your thoughts? What you write on Facebook? Do others see Christ in your life? At work? With your family? Your whole life should make God look good. Too often Christians bring disrepute to the name of Christ.

³² Do not cause anyone to stumble, whether Jews, Greeks or the church of God.

6. Will this cause someone to stumble? Always seek to build others up in your words and deeds, whether it is your wife, a Christian brother, or someone of another religion. Never do anything that will cause them to stumble. It is an integral part of acting in love.

³³ I, too, try to please everyone in everything I do. I don't just do what is best for me; I do what is best for others so that many may be saved. (NLT)

7. Do I have a heart that wants to please those around me? To help them? Or am I only thinking about my own interests? Am I acting in a way that will draw them to the Savior? That doesn't mean we are to be "man pleasers." We want to please God, but because we are fighting selfishness and seeking to love others, we want to please them also. Do everything possible to help your church and community, and point others to Jesus.

¹¹:¹ Follow my example, as I follow the example of Christ.

8. Is there an example to follow? Jesus? Your pastor? Biblical characters? Other mature believers? What kind of example do you give? Several years ago everyone was asking "What would Jesus do?" Christ is always our best example. Study the Gospels and follow that example. Thankfully, Christ also gives us mature Christians here on earth to follow. Can you tell a younger Christian: Follow me? Are you following Christ in all of your life?

Be sure to apply each of these principles before making your decision. Ask the Holy Spirit to help you and wait for his confirmation, or pay close attention to any check in your spirit as you start to act on a decision. Be careful of others who are living under the law, trying to follow man-made rules. But at the same time, while we reject legalism, carefully apply each of these guidelines to all areas of your life. For example, in the past some churches had strict rules about women's dress. But in rejecting that legalism, women may cause their brothers to stumble with their revealing clothes.

17

God's Order for Men and Women
1 Corinthians 11:2-16

This is a controversial passage, one which frequently is cited as the most difficult in all of Paul's epistles. We know that some things in the Bible were customs of that time; for example, what Paul says about women cutting their hair or covering their head. But how do we know which principles are eternal? There still are churches which forbid women to cut their hair. And there are churches that believe the order that God established for men and women was simply part of the culture of that day, and doesn't apply to us. We need the Holy Spirit to free us from confusion, give us wisdom, and guide us into the truth as we seek to apply this teaching to the twenty-first century.

[2] I praise you for remembering me in everything and for holding to the traditions just as I passed them on to you. [3] But I want you to realize that the head of every man is Christ, and the head of the woman is man, and the head of Christ is God. [4] Every man who prays or prophesies with his head covered dishonors his head. [5] But every woman who prays or prophesies with her head uncovered dishonors her head—it is the same as having her head shaved. [6] For if a woman does not cover her head, she might as well have her hair cut off; but if it is a disgrace for a woman to

have her hair cut off or her head shaved, then she should cover her head.

The Meaning of "Headship"

Many believers feel uncomfortable with this passage and the idea that a woman has a "head," but it is not helpful to explain away what "head" obviously means, nor is it our place to pick and choose what we feel comfortable with in the Bible. It is very clear what "head" (Greek: *kephale*) means:

- In our bodies it is the head that directs all the bodily functions.
- In government or industry, the head is the one in charge.
- Verse 3, consistent with other Biblical teaching, speaks of the authority God has established in the world.
- Reading the Gospels, it is evident that Jesus submitted to his Father in everything, which is how he in turn received his authority (see Matthew 8:8-10).
- In Ephesians 5:22-28 Paul uses the same word ("head"), clearly linking it to female submission and male authority.

Christ found joy and fulfillment in the freedom of submission to his Father.

- In the same way that the Father is his head, Christ is the head of man, and man is the head of woman.
- The man must submit to Christ in everything, and finds freedom, fulfillment, and joy in that submission.
- The woman submits to man and finds the freedom to be fulfilled in her family. That doesn't mean that she cannot

work or do ministry. Women have the freedom to pray or prophesy in the church – if it is done in order.

- The point of verses 4 and 5 is the importance of honoring the one God has placed as our head. At that time (but generally not today), a covered head was a sign of submission.

Headship has nothing to do with men being better than women. Father, Son, and Spirit are equally God – but only function in their proper order. The universe functions with remarkable order; the planets don't rebel against the places designated for them. That same order is necessary for society to properly function; anarchy doesn't work. Our nation's families and schools give ample evidence of what happens when that order breaks down.

Being the head carries great responsibility. Authority has a very negative connotation today, but it is central to biblical faith. We must submit to it and teach it in our churches. It is not about dominating anyone, but rather about serving, to free others to be all God made them to be. Read Watchman Nee's *Spiritual Authority* for further study and reflection.

Male/Female Relationships

[7] A man ought not to cover his head, since he is the image and glory of God; but woman is the glory of man. [8] For man did not come from woman, but woman from man; [9] neither was man created for woman, but woman for man. [10] It is for this reason that a woman ought to have authority over her own head, because of the angels. [11] Nevertheless, in the Lord woman is not independent of man, nor is man independent of woman. [12] For as woman came from man, so also man is born of woman. But everything comes from God.

13 Judge for yourselves: Is it proper for a woman to pray to God with her head uncovered? 14 Does not the very nature of things teach you that if a man has long hair, it is a disgrace to him, 15 but that if a woman has long hair, it is her glory? For long hair is given to her as a covering. 16 If anyone wants to be contentious about this, we have no other practice—nor do the churches of God.

Paul's teaching on the relationship between men and women is grounded in creation:

- Man is the image and glory of God; woman is the glory of man (7). Male and female together are the image of God.

- The man reflects God's nature and should bring glory to his Creator, so that others will praise God.

- The woman reflects her husband. A woman who is loved by her husband shines, and others will note that she has a husband who loves and cares for her. The husband is responsible for presenting her as a radiant bride to the Lord (Ephesians 5:27).

- Man did not come from woman. Woman came from man (8). In creation, Adam was formed from the dust of the ground, but Eve from Adam's rib.

- Man was not created for woman, rather the woman was created for man (9), as a suitable helpmate and companion.

These are universal principles, but for those in Christ, there is something more. Man is not independent of woman, nor is woman independent of man (11); man is born of woman, and both come from God. Nobody is superior. We need each other. Independence and the loss of relationship distort our human experience. In Christ, women are lifted to an equality unknown in the ancient world, redeemed from the curse, and restored to God's original intention as a suitable helpmate.

Warning!

This is not a blank check for a man to be harsh in his home or abuse his wife. Unfortunately, many Christian men don't demonstrate much love or respect for their wives, which has caused some women to rebel and reject the Bible as outdated. Christ is the example of headship. He was not harsh or demanding with his disciples. He said that the greatest must be the servant of all. God commands husbands to love their wives as Christ loves the church, and gave himself for her (Ephesians 5:25). Christ's example is one of self-sacrifice and service. Women are weaker vessels, and we must treasure them.

I know the teaching of this chapter goes against the grain. Extensive study has been done on this passage, and many serious Bible scholars would disagree with me. It is fine if you don't agree, but try to put aside your twenty-first century American mind set for a moment, and carefully and prayerfully study what the Bible actually says.

18

Spiritual Gifts

1 Corinthians 12

Now to each one the manifestation of the Spirit is given for the common good (7).

To each one

Have you ever been at a Christmas party where everyone receives gifts...except you? It feels bad. Thank God, you never have to feel that way with the Lord. He gives gifts to every Christian. *To each one* means...you! If you have the Holy Spirit, God gives you a gift.

Open it! Use it!

If you receive a gift, don't you want to open it? I suspect if you were given a new iPad you would waste no time turning it on and using it. How is it, then, that God has far better gifts, which will truly help our brothers and sisters, and we ignore them, abuse them, and don't bother learning how to use them?

God needs you!

Isn't it amazing that the God of the universe has chosen to rely on us to prepare his Son's bride? God is trying to build a strong church, but he needs every member to do their part. Anyone not using his gift is robbing the church of a blessing - and is in sin. Do you know what your gift is? Are you using it? When was the last time you experienced a *manifestation of the Spirit* that blessed your church?

Don't be uninformed

Now about the gifts of the Spirit, brothers and sisters, I do not want you to be uninformed or misinformed (1).

Unfortunately, many are both. What is a spiritual gift? It is simply a *manifestation of the Spirit* (7). A gift has nothing to do with your natural talents; it is God supernaturally working through your life, for the benefit of his church. If you are quenching the Spirit, denying his power, or full of yourself instead of the Spirit, he can't manifest himself. If your church tries to control the Spirit or doesn't expect anything supernatural, gifts probably will not be manifest.

Of course you also must be saved. That is why Paul emphasizes that these gifts have nothing to do with their former idolatry:

² You know that when you were pagans, somehow or other you were influenced and led astray to mute idols. ³ Therefore I want you to know that no one who is speaking by the Spirit of God says, "Jesus be cursed," and no one can say, "Jesus is Lord," except by the Holy Spirit.

As opposed to mute idols, the Spirit speaks. The first evidence of the Spirit's presence in our lives is our confession of Jesus as Lord, and most manifestations of the Spirit involve speaking. The Spirit's work is always constructive; he will never curse Jesus or harm his body.

The first characteristic of the Body of Christ: Diversity

*There are different kinds of gifts, but the **same Spirit** distributes them. (4)*
*There are different kinds of service, but the **same Lord**. (5)*
*There are different kinds of working, but in all of them and in everyone it is the **same God** at work. (6)*

The Trinity demonstrates what God intends for the church: perfect unity, but with diverse functions. In these three verses Paul parallels the Holy Spirit, the Lord Jesus, and God the Father, confirming the divinity and equality of each member of the Trinity.

All these are the work of one and the same Spirit, and he distributes them to each one, just as he determines (11).

Though there is great diversity in the gifts, they all flow from one source, the Holy Spirit. Verse 1 of chapter 14 tells us to desire gifts, and even seek after certain gifts. The last verse of chapter 12 says: *Now eagerly desire the greater gifts* (31). Yet it is still the Spirit who determines what you receive. He knows what the church needs, he knows you completely, and he distributes the gifts perfectly, just as he wants.

Some of the gifts

Two lists of gifts are given in this chapter, with some gifts appearing on both. Other lists are found in Romans 12:6-8,

Ephesians 4:11, and 1 Peter 4:11. These lists don't seem to be exhaustive, but rather examples of common manifestations of gifts.

⁸ To one there is given through the Spirit a message of wisdom, to another a message of knowledge by means of the same Spirit, ⁹ to another faith by the same Spirit, to another gifts of healing by that one Spirit, ¹⁰ to another miraculous powers, to another prophecy, to another distinguishing between spirits, to another speaking in different kinds of tongues, and to still another the interpretation of tongues.

²⁸ And God has placed in the church first of all apostles, second prophets, third teachers, then miracles, then gifts of healing, of helping, of guidance, and of different kinds of tongues. ²⁹ Are all apostles? Are all prophets? Are all teachers? Do all work miracles? ³⁰ Do all have gifts of healing? Do all speak in tongues? Do all interpret?

There is a hierarchy of gifts; Paul mentions *greater gifts.*

- Apostles are in first place, as a foundation for the church.

- Prophets follow. What a shame many churches don't recognize these two foundational gifts! Is it any surprise the church is weak?

- Paul doesn't mention evangelists or pastors, though they are part of the five ministry offices in Ephesians four. Here he puts teachers in third place, followed by those who work miracles.

We need to submit to God, gratefully accepting whatever gift he gives us. Don't envy those with "greater gifts." The obvious answer to the question "Does everyone have certain gifts?" is "no." The same Spirit is at work, but there is great diversity in the gifts.

I have seen a lot of confusion about what the gifts mean. They are supernatural abilities which you cannot perform in your own strength. When "spiritual gift inventories" are completed, hardly anyone ends up with "miraculous" gifts. If you believe those inventories, there would be great imbalance in the body. My suspicion is that much that passes for "gifts" are actually natural talents.

There is no definitive definition of each gifts, but here are some thoughts:

- *Apostle*: Has authority to establish and oversee churches.
- *Prophecy*: The spiritual gift (which we will study in detail in chapter 14) differs from the *office* of prophet, which is similar to the Old Testament prophet. That is not confined to one church, but brings words directly from the Lord to build up and guide various churches.
- *Word of wisdom*: The ability to analyze a situation and offer a supernatural solution; very helpful in counseling.
- *Word of knowledge*: Ability to see "inside" a person or situation and know what is happening; similar to prophecy.
- *Faith*: Every Christian needs saving faith; the person with this gift will have great visions of what God can do, and the faith to make it happen.
- *Healing*: We can all pray for someone's healing, but the person with the gift of healing will be known for remarkable and consistent healing abilities.
- *Miracles*: Such as raising the dead or multiplying food.
- *Discerning of spirits*: Very important to discern the

presence of demons, false doctrine, or false prophecy. Is able to see beyond appearances.

- *Speaking in tongues and interpreting tongues*. We will learn about these gifts in chapter 14.

- *Helps*: We should all be helping others, but the person with this gift can motivate the church to great works of service. I think of those who built hospitals in the past, or the founder of World Vision.

- *Guidance (administration)*: A special ability to analyze a situation in the church and organize it to run efficiently and smoothly.

Many times someone will have complementary gifts, such as healing with word of knowledge, or faith with miracles. I don't see biblical evidence that the gifts become our "possession," so that we necessarily operate in the same gift for life. That may often be the case, but since it is the Spirit's manifestation, it could change according to the need of the church.

If we are to function as Christ intended us to, we need all these manifestations of the Spirit. Open your heart for the Lord to speak to you about gifts in your life and church. With something so important, I am confident he will guide you if you are truly open.

19

You are the Body of Christ

1 Corinthians 12

Now you are the body of Christ, and each one of you is a part of it (27).

Paul summarizes some of the Bible's clearest teaching on the church with this astonishing statement. It is not a social club or religious organization, nor is it something you choose to join. When you accept Jesus into your life you become a part of his body. It is very hard to be a true Christian all by yourself - our faith involves a relationship with God and other believers. Jesus no longer walks this earth, but his body is everywhere. Miraculously, there are millions of local expressions of Christ's body all over the world. If they follow God's plan, with each member in its place manifesting gifts of the Holy Spirit, each church has the capacity to do what Jesus did.

12 Just as a body, though one, has many parts, but all its many parts form one body, so it is with Christ. 13 For we were all baptized by one Spirit so as to form one body—whether Jews or Gentiles, slave or free—and we were all given the one Spirit to drink.

God uses something each of us is intimately familiar with to help us understand the unity and diversity of the church: our bodies. For your body to function properly, every member must do its part, working together with the other members. There would be chaos if they did not obey the head (your brain), or, in the church, Jesus Christ. Jesus' blood (spiritually) flows through his whole body, purifying it and bringing nutrients to each member.

Unity in the body

Unity flows from our common experience of the Holy Spirit, in baptism (in the Spirit, water, or both), and drinking of his fullness. The Spirit is like water, the essential life force. The body won't function if everyone is not drinking of the Spirit.

- There is absolute equality in the body. There is no difference between black and white, rich and poor, or powerful and humble. The Spirit erases all those divisions in a bond of love. Any kind of prejudice is sin, which destroys the church and grieves its Lord.

- This unity and diversity is so important that Paul repeats it twice more:

    o *Even so the body is not made up of one part but of many* (14).

    o *As it is, there are many parts, but one body (20).*

- The body is expressed in local congregations as well as in the church universal worldwide.

Jesus prayed for the unity of his body in John 17, and we can assume his prayers are powerful! Satan obviously is intent on dividing the church, so we must be on guard and do everything possible to maintain its unity.

¹⁵ Now if the foot should say, "Because I am not a hand, I do not belong to the body," it would not for that reason stop being part of the body.¹⁶ And if the ear should say, "Because I am not an eye, I do not belong to the body," it would not for that reason stop being part of the body.¹⁷ If the whole body were an eye, where would the sense of hearing be? If the whole body were an ear, where would the sense of smell be? ¹⁸ But in fact God has placed the parts in the body, every one of them, just as he wanted them to be. ¹⁹ If they were all one part, where would the body be?

Just as your foot can't decide it is tired of being stepped on all the time, you can't simply decide you no longer want to be part of Christ's body. Rebellion is not allowed. Have you ever watched one of those shows on how our bodies work? The complexity is absolutely amazing! I don't see how anyone could think it just happened or evolved: *"In him we live and move and have our being"* (Acts 17:28). It is a miracle of God that something so complex works smoothly (more or less) for some eighty years. The church is just as complex, and just as dependent on God to function.

We need each member!

Unfortunately, all the hands tend to gather in one place, all the feet in another, and on it goes - resulting in a dysfunctional, deformed, body. Contrary to what Paul says about us needing each other, hands often feel they are better than feet and don't need them, so we end up with cripples who can't walk and certainly do not reflect the glorious presence of Jesus Christ. We must accept all the gifts and the many expressions of the body, and discern where God wishes to place the members. Questioning how he has placed the members is tantamount to saying God doesn't know how to build a church.

[21] The eye cannot say to the hand, "I don't need you!" And the head cannot say to the feet, "I don't need you!" [22] On the contrary, those parts of the body that seem to be weaker are indispensable, [23] and the parts that we think are less honorable we treat with special honor. And the parts that are unpresentable are treated with special modesty, [24] while our presentable parts need no special treatment. But God has put the body together, giving greater honor to the parts that lacked it, [25] so that there should be no division in the body, but that its parts should have equal concern for each other.

This is common sense – but unfortunately many Christians fail to grasp the importance of this simple teaching. If you have ever hurt your foot you know it impacts your whole life. Each part of our bodies has an important function; you can't say one is more important than the other. There is amazing coordination among the various parts, but if they start fighting each other, your body will break down. Are you familiar with auto-immune diseases, where your body's defenses attack your own body? What a shame that it afflicts the body of Christ!

Each member should show true concern for the other members, recognizing their unique value. If we allow God to put the body together as he wants it, division should be rare.

God delights in doing things contrary to our expectations, giving special honor to the parts others tend to look down on. Do you think some members of the body are less important? God says they are indispensable! We take special care of the intimate parts of our bodies. In the same way, special treatment should be given to members of the church that seem less honorable.

If one part suffers, every part suffers with it; if one part is honored, every part rejoices with it (26).

In the church nobody should silently suffer alone. We need to genuinely share in each other's suffering, and even though it may be hard to do while you are going through trials, rejoice with those who are honored. To do that you must know what is happening in their lives.

On a world-wide level, if Jesus' body is suffering in another country, we need to share in their suffering. We will see Paul's great concern for that in chapter sixteen. That means we make it our business to know what is going on in other places. It is sinful for us to go on living the good life while brothers and sisters in other countries are suffering.

What has your experience been in the church?

This is basic, simple, teaching on the church. It is vital to being a healthy Christian, yet in forty years serving the Lord I have seldom seen it working. Why? Why does it seem so hard for us to follow through on Jesus' simple plan for his church? Is it because Satan knows how powerful a healthy church would be?

The chapter ends with these words: *And yet I will show you the most excellent way* (31). Amazing as this teaching on the body and its gifts is, there is something even better, essential to making it work.

20

Becoming a Man
1 Corinthians 13

This is better than gifts and miracles and the abundant life. This is *the most excellent way*: love. This is one of the most beloved and well known chapters of the Bible. If chapters twelve and fourteen were the bread in a sandwich, this would be the filling. Without love those chapters can become mechanical and tasteless; biology with no heart. Sadly, it seems we have missed the message. God is love. A church without love is really not a church. *Whoever claims to love God yet hates a brother or sister is a liar. For whoever does not love their brother and sister, whom they have seen, cannot love God, whom they have not seen* (1 John 4:20; read that whole letter for some of the Bible's richest insights on love).

The Greek word Paul uses for love throughout this chapter is *agape*, God's unconditional love. This isn't the love between a man and a woman, or fraternal love. *Agape* is an active love, a love that few know. It is not optional for the Christian: The first commandment is to love God with all your heart, and the second is to love your neighbor as yourself.

Love is a fruit of the Spirit. God teaches us how to love, because *agape* is impossible without God's help. The Bible says we love because he first loved us (1 John 4:19). In God's plan, a child should experience love at home and learn to love from his parents' example. But we know there are no perfect parents, and too many have never experienced a father's love. It is only in relationship with God that we can experience true *agape* love. The other problem is that many of us don't love ourselves, making it difficult to love others. In that relationship with God we learn that we are made according to his image, we are of infinite value to God, and he has a great purpose for our lives. God forgives us and frees us from those things that could cause us to hate ourselves. He also gives us many opportunities to learn how to love, especially with people who are hard to love. Jesus said even the worst sinners love those who love them (Matthew 5:43-48); he commands us to love our enemies, which is only possible with *agape* love.

More important than the gifts

Paul continues the theme of spiritual gifts from chapter 12, purposely choosing some of the most impressive things a Christian could do – only to say that without love they are worthless. Since they were obsessed with tongues, he starts there. Tongues are an amazing gift – it is the language of angels - but without love they are just noise, and God is not impressed. In their zeal, at times tongues-speakers have lacked love.

[1]If I speak in the tongues of men or of angels, but do not have love, I am only a resounding gong or a clanging cymbal. [2] If I have the gift of prophecy and can fathom all mysteries and all knowledge, and if I have a faith that can move mountains, but do not have love, I am nothing. [3] If I give all I possess to the poor and give over my body to hardship that I may boast, but do not have love, I gain nothing.

He also speaks of gifts of prophecy, words of knowledge and wisdom (fathoming mysteries), faith, and helping others. You can have the greatest gifts and use them to the extreme, but they mean nothing if you don't have love. Love always takes priority in the use of gifts in the church. Self-denial and even martyrdom gain you nothing if they don't flow from *agape* love.

What is love?

We tend to think of it as a warm feeling of attraction to someone who makes us feel good, often with sexual overtones. Co-dependency and the euphoria of "being in love" can be mistaken for true love.

The dictionary doesn't help us much, offering these definitions:

- A strong positive emotion of regard and affection.
- A deep feeling of sexual desire and attraction.
- Any object of warm affection or devotion.
- Or how about: A score of zero in tennis or squash!

These definitions are vague, and all about feelings, which as we know can change quickly. Thankfully, true love is far deeper and longer lasting.

Biblical love

4 Love is patient, love is kind. It does not envy, it does not boast, it is not proud. 5 It does not dishonor others, it is not self-seeking, it is not easily angered, it keeps no record of wrongs. 6 Love does not delight in evil but rejoices with the truth. 7 It always protects, always trusts, always hopes, always perseveres.

Love is:

- Patient (never gives up)

- Kind (cares more for others than for self)

Love always:

- Protects (puts up with anything).

- Trusts (is ready to believe the best of every person).

- Hopes (under all circumstances, never looking back).

- Perseveres (endures everything without weakening, keeps going to the end).

- Rejoices with the truth (is always truthful and happy when truth wins out).

Love does not:

- Envy (covet, want what it doesn't have).

- Boast (focus on self and how great you are).

- Keep a record of wrongs (takes no account of the evil done to it, pays no attention to a wrong suffered).

- Delight in evil (injustice).

- Fail. Ever. (It will last forever.)

Love is not:

- Proud   Rude (forcing itself on others).

- Self-seeking (insisting on its own rights or own way).

- Easily angered (touchy, fretful, or resentful).

Do you love in this way? Is this love present in your home? Your church? If not, what needs to change? Have you failed in truly loving others? Do you need to repent of that? Is it possible your lack of love has damaged your family, your church, and your relationship with God?

When perfection comes

8 Love never fails. But where there are prophecies, they will cease; where there are tongues, they will be stilled; where there is knowledge, it will pass away. 9 For we know in part and we prophesy in part, 10 but when completeness comes, what is in part disappears. 11 When I was a child, I talked like a child, I thought like a child, I reasoned like a child. When I became a man, I put the ways of childhood behind me. 12 For now we see only a reflection as in a mirror; then we shall see face to face. Now I know in part; then I shall know fully, even as I am fully known.

Some have manipulated these verses to say that prophecy and tongues (and even knowledge!) ended when "completeness" (or perfection) arrived, which they say was found in the completion of the New Testament. But we are not seeing the Lord face to face yet. Completion and perfection come with Jesus' return; in his presence we won't need those gifts. Meanwhile, don't expect perfection in your marriage, your church, or your own ministry. It is not possible. Be merciful with others' imperfections. Better than focusing on those imperfections, think about seeing Christ face to face. Are you ready, or will your face be covered with shame? How amazing to think of the perfect knowledge God has of you – and the same knowledge you will have! How great to know that the imperfection we experience now will disappear!

Man or boy?

You expect a child to talk, think, and reason like a child. That's good. But there is a problem if you don't give up your childish ways when you become a man. How about you? Are you holding on to some childish ways? Have you "become a man"? God wants you to, and Paul thinks there is a point at which it should happen. Unfortunately, many never seem to make it. Are there ways you still talk, think, or reason like a child? What does that look like? How is a man supposed to talk, think, and reason? Paul certainly is saying that one of the key marks of true manhood is loving as he describes here. Every man knows how to make love – but few know how to love. Are you more of a boy, or a man?

And now these three remain: faith, hope and love. But the greatest of these is love (13).

How is your hope? Have you given up hope for much happening in your life, marriage, or church? How is your faith? And most important, your love? Make it your priority to be a man of love. It is wonderful to do great things for the Lord, but the greatest is love. Study what this chapter teaches about love. Meditate on it. Make it part of your life. Study all the Bible teaches about love. *We love because God first loved us* (1 John 4:19). Have you experienced his love? If you haven't, it will be almost impossible to love like this. Open your heart to him and ask him to fill you with his love.

21

Prophecy
1 Corinthians 14

Follow the way of love and eagerly desire gifts of the Spirit, especially prophecy (1).

Tongues and prophecy.
Misunderstood.
Despised.
Over rated.
Ignored.
Abused.
And they're just gifts God has given his church to help us hear him and communicate with him! Something any Christian needs and wants!

Follow (Amplified: *make you aim, your great quest*) *the way of love.* The Greek word the NIV translates *follow* implies dedicating yourself and your time to eagerly pursuing and seeking to acquire an objective. Is that your attitude toward love?

Eagerly (intensely) *desire* (and cultivate) *gifts of the Spirit,* like a child intensely desires that Christmas gift. Is that how you feel about spiritual gifts? Do you give them much thought? Most people eagerly desire their own blessings more than gifts that benefit the whole church. They are very important to God; they are his way of equipping and building his Body. Think about the time, effort, and money we put into food and body building!

Especially prophecy. Of all the gifts, prophecy may be most important. Paul's emphasis on it would certainly make sense to early Christians with Jewish backgrounds. The Old Testament prophets were spiritual men who impacted the whole nation with messages they received directly from the Lord. The Jews had just emerged from hundreds of years of prophetic silence. Early believers would have been appalled at the idea that God might no longer speak. With salvation in Christ and the outpouring of the Spirit they would expect prophecy to be even more common, as Joel 2:28 predicted. Amazingly, every Christian could hear God's voice and prophesy!

² For anyone who speaks in a tongue does not speak to people but to God. Indeed, no one understands them; they utter mysteries by the Spirit. ³ But the one who prophesies speaks to people for their strengthening, encouraging and comfort. ⁴ Anyone who speaks in a tongue edifies themselves, but the one who prophesies edifies the church. ⁵ I would like every one of you to speak in tongues, but I would rather have you prophesy. The one who prophesies is greater than the one who speaks in tongues, unless someone interprets, so that the church may be edified.

We will study tongues in the next chapter. Here Paul compares the two to show prophecy is superior because it builds up the whole church, so that everyone can grow spiritually (a message in tongues which is interpreted is the same as prophecy). Paul wishes that *everyone* would prophesy.

The purpose of prophecy

- Strengthen or edify.

- Comfort, or console.

- Encourage or exhort: Some people think of exhorting as rebuking, but that is not the meaning here. The Greek word is *paraklesis*, related to the word *paraklete*, used for the Holy Spirit. Like the Spirit, the one prophesying comes alongside to comfort and encourage.

The person functioning in the *office* of prophet may bring predictions about the future or revelation about sin in the church (as in the letters in Revelation 2 and 3), but that is not the purpose of the *gift* of prophecy. Instead of rebuking or judging others, prophecy should build up.

Prophecy as a sign for believers

[21] *In the Law it is written:*
"With other tongues
   and through the lips of foreigners
I will speak to this people,
   but even then they will not listen to me,
says the Lord."
[22] *Tongues, then, are a sign, not for believers but for unbelievers; prophecy, however, is not for unbelievers but for believers.* [23] *So if the whole church comes together and everyone speaks in tongues, and inquirers or unbelievers come in, will they not say that you are out of your mind?* [24] *But if an unbeliever or an inquirer comes in while everyone is prophesying, they are convicted of sin and are brought under judgment by all,* [25] *as the secrets of their hearts are laid bare. So they will fall down and worship God, exclaiming, "God is really among you!"*

This is a difficult passage. If unbelievers who hear everyone speaking in tongues think they are crazy, why does Paul say tongues are a sign for unbelievers? It is because the verses he quotes from Isaiah (28:11-12) refer to unbelieving *Israelites*; not someone who has no knowledge of God.

When an unbeliever hears prophecy in a church service:

- The secrets of his heart can be exposed.

- He may be convicted of sin and overwhelmed by the supernatural presence of God.

- As a result he may fall down and worship!

Procedures for using the gift in church

When Paul speaks of *everyone* prophesying, it is clear that the whole church could be involved:

²⁹ Two or three prophets should speak, and the others should weigh carefully what is said. ³⁰ And if a revelation comes to someone who is sitting down, the first speaker should stop. ³¹ For you can all prophesy in turn so that everyone may be instructed and encouraged. ³² The spirits of prophets are subject to the control of prophets. ³³ For God is not a God of disorder but of peace—as in all the congregations of the Lord's people.

To understand this passage we must be clear on the difference between the *gift* of prophecy and the *office* of prophet. Paul already said that all are not *prophets*, but he wishes that everyone would *prophesy*. Only two or three *prophets* are to speak, but everyone with the *gift of prophecy* can speak in turn (as Paul also said in verse 24). To have the gift of prophecy doesn't necessarily make you a prophet.

Possibly these verses could be read like this (my own amplified translation):

Regarding those who hold the office of prophet, two or three should speak, while the others (anyone in the church, but especially those with the gift of discernment of spirits; possibly the other prophets) should carefully weigh what is said. If someone with the gift of prophecy receives a revelation while they are seated, the prophet who is speaking should stop and allow them to share the word. In that way everyone with the gift of prophecy can speak in turn so that everyone may be instructed and encouraged. The gift of prophecy, and those who operate in that gift, are under the control of those in the office of prophet, because God is not a God of disorder but of peace.

This is one possible interpretation of a difficult passage. In this scenario, prophecies could take considerable time in a worship service, and obviously could not be programmed. Once again we see that those operating in the gift of prophecy are not predicting the future, but offering *instruction and encouragement*. Their words come by *revelation*, but Paul recognizes the possibility of some words not being truly inspired; thus the requirement for every prophetic word to be evaluated.

Summary

There is very little teaching in the New Testament on using this gift, possibly because it was so common. Despite the difficulties with this passage, several things are very clear:

- There is an office of prophet, is second in authority after apostles (1 Corinthians 12:28). The prophet is also second in the five-fold ministries in Ephesians 4:11.

- There is a gift of prophecy which all can receive, distinct from the office of prophet as a ministry.
- Paul portrays this gift as highly important; opportunity should be provided in every service for its manifestation.
- Prophecy is for instruction and encouragement.
- Prophecy must function within the safety of the church. The person exercising the gift should be known by the church leadership and operate under their authority. Be very careful of prophets on the internet or ministering out of some back room. If prophecy isn't balanced by the other gifts in the body there is great risk of abuse.
- Every prophetic word should be tested.
- There is no need to fear losing your word because you have to wait a few moments to share it, but if someone else with the gift receives a revelation while you are speaking, you are to give them the opportunity to speak. A prophet does not lose self-control.
- We need to develop discernment about what to share. God may give you words that are not intended to be shared with the whole church.
- If there is a lack of order or peace we need to question if it is really of the Lord.
- Some still teach that the gift of prophecy is simply teaching or preaching the Bible, but it is clear from this chapter that is Spirit-inspired speech.
- A true prophetic word will never contradict the Bible, and should never be taken with the same authority as the Bible.

Your experience with prophecy

Here are some thoughts that may be helpful in using this gift:

- We no longer stone false prophets as they did in the Old Testament, and nowhere does it say that perfection is required to be a prophet. If a prophecy is tested and found lacking it is simply stated that we sense the word is not from the Lord, in such a way that the person who gave it isn't humiliated. However, when a "prophet" repeatedly gives words that don't come to pass (as I have frequently observed on the internet or in churches), I believe the church has a responsibility to express concern about their ministry. Too often those "prophets" keep going with no accountability to anyone. At the same time, we need to remember that prophecy about a coming judgment or disaster may be given to awaken us to intercede so that God may mercifully spare us. In that case the predicted tragedy may be avoided.

- A prophetic word will often be sparked by a scripture, a single word, an image, or simply a feeling. For example, you may have a strong feeling of heaviness, sadness, or love. You might start by saying: "I sense that God's heart is very heavy." You don't know why at the moment, but you start speaking in faith. As you speak, the Lord may give you more: "Some of you are struggling under condemnation from the devil because of sin in your past." Now the words start to flow: "The Lord says that Jesus died for your sins and has already paid the price. God has forgotten about those sins and loves you. He wants to set you free from that condemnation right now." If the word is from the Lord, simply speaking it forth may result in release for those who were struggling.

- You may feel a fullness, like something is rising up through your throat that must be expressed.

- Sometimes a word you give may spark a word in someone else and the message will grow from person to person.

- It is usually better not to say "Thus says the Lord," or use an exaggerated tone with King James English. It seems better to say: "I believe the Lord wants to say…" or "I'm sensing in my heart…"

- We want to create an atmosphere of expectancy and safety in the church that encourages people to prophesy. It should be natural and common. It may be easier to start in a small group. After prayer or worship the leader may ask: "Does anyone sense something from the Lord in their spirit?" Worship often prepares us to hear from the Lord as we wait in his presence. Leave enough time for the Lord to speak. Don't quench the Spirit because you feel uncomfortable with a lengthy silence.

- Be careful of it becoming so routine that a few trusty "prophets" feel they must always come up with some word. There are internet sites where a "prophet" supposedly receives a new word every day. I am suspicious of them; God does not operate according to our schedules.

- Teach your church how to bring forth a prophetic word.

- o Some pastors prefer that the person clears it with a leader before sharing it.
- o In a large church a microphone may be needed.
- o Explain what is happening, and if a word is judged not to be from the Lord, express that gently, and with love.

[39] Therefore, my brothers and sisters, be eager to prophesy, and do not forbid speaking in tongues. [40] But everything should be done in a fitting and orderly way.

How well do you and your church reflect the Scriptural view of prophecy? Do you eagerly desire to experience it? Unfortunately, prophetic words are rare in many churches that supposedly are open to the work of the Spirit. If there is prophecy in your church, is it done in a fitting and orderly way that truly edifies the body? Some have rejected prophecy because it created problems in the past. That is simply a failure on the part of church leadership to make sure it is exercised within the loving limits of pastoral authority. What a privilege to hear from the living God today! I pray that you and your church would fully benefit from this wonderful gift.

22

"I would like every one of you to speak in tongues." (Paul)
1 Corinthians 14

I would like every one of you to speak in tongues (5).

I thank God that I speak in tongues more than all of you (18).

Do not forbid speaking in tongues (39).

Paul obviously thought speaking in tongues was valuable, so why is it still such a sensitive subject? Certainly it has been abused and overemphasized, as was the case in Corinth, but Paul doesn't respond by suggesting that they stop using it. In fact, he wishes they would all speak in tongues! You don't reject something God has given just because it has been misused. You seek a biblical balance! Those who vehemently speak against the gift are those who don't have it. I have never heard anyone who prays in tongues say it is worthless or not of God.

Tongues certainly is not a major biblical theme. Mark 16:17 is the only Gospel reference, and that is part of a passage the NIV says is not included in the "earliest manuscripts and some other ancient witnesses." There Jesus says that tongues is a sign that will accompany those who believe, along with snake handling and drinking poison. Whether the passage is authentic or not, tongues was probably so common in the early church that they only wrote about it in connection with the abuses in Corinth.

There is an interesting connection between tongues and prophecy (see Acts 19:6). Several times in the Old Testament when the Spirit fell they prophesied (Numbers 11:25-27, 1 Samuel 10:5-13; 18:10; 19:20-24). It appears to be an ecstatic praise similar to tongues, because it is clear they were not proclaiming messages received from the Lord.

Is tongues the sign of Spirit baptism?

Some believe that tongues is the necessary sign of Spirit baptism, or that you are not even saved if you don't speak in tongues. Since much of the controversy has centered on this teaching, we will look at the three times in Acts when they spoke in tongues after being baptized in the Spirit:

Acts 2:4: *All of them were filled with the Holy Spirit and began to speak in other tongues as the Spirit enabled them.*

At Pentecost *all of them* were filled and *all of them* spoke in tongues. Based on what happened there, some insist genuine tongues are foreign languages. God obviously can give someone knowledge of a language they never learned; I have heard of that happening. But aside from the fact Paul says tongues are mysteries which no one can understand, there are several reasons I believe the tongues on Pentecost were not foreign languages:

- Four times it says the crowd *heard* them speaking in their own language. This was a double miracle, where God effectively provided translation to the hearers. That is why they were bewildered, amazed and perplexed.
- There were 120 people speaking loud enough to draw a crowd, and fifteen people groups mentioned. A simple experiment with that many people loudly speaking that many languages will show that no one would have been able to understand anything.
- The disciples were acting and speaking in such a way that others thought they were drunk.

Acts 10: 45-46: *The circumcised believers who had come with Peter were astonished that the gift of the Holy Spirit had been poured out even on Gentiles. For they heard them speaking in tongues and praising God.*

It was tongues that convinced the Jews that they had received the Spirit. It is interesting that Peter doesn't mention the tongues when he later recounts what happened, perhaps because everyone assumed they would have spoken in tongues.

Acts 19:6: *When Paul placed his hands on them, the Holy Spirit came on them, and they spoke in tongues and prophesied.*

The only place where tongues *and* prophecy are mentioned as a result of initially receiving the Spirit, this may be like the Old Testament prophecy I mentioned above.

There is only one other Spirit baptism recorded in Acts (8:17). Something attracted Simon's attention that made him want the ability to baptize people. It could be tongues, though they are not mentioned. Are three out of four events enough to form a doctrine that tongues *must* be the sign of Spirit baptism? Scripture never teaches that, although it is safe to say the result of baptism in the Spirit is speaking forth God's praises, *usually* in tongues, and when it was received everyone experienced it. To make it *the* sign, however, seems to go against 1 Corinthians 14:22: *Tongues, then, are a sign, not for believers but for unbelievers.*

The purpose of tongues

² For anyone who speaks in a tongue does not speak to people but to God. Indeed, no one understands them; they utter mysteries by the Spirit.

When you pray in tongues, the third person of the Trinity dwelling in your heart communicates directly with the Lord. They may be mysteries, but many times I have a sense of what I am praying about. This is obviously a great advantage in prayer, since you are always praying God's will, and can intercede for the needs of family and others who are far away.

⁴ Anyone who speaks in a tongue edifies themselves, but the one who prophesies edifies the church. ⁵ I would like every one of you to speak in tongues, but I would rather have you prophesy. The one who prophesies is greater than the one who speaks in tongues, unless someone interprets, so that the church may be edified.

The advantage of prophecy is that it blesses the whole church, but there is nothing wrong with edifying yourself! Far from making it self-centered and worthless (as some have claimed), it is an amazing God-given provision to build yourself up in the

Spirit any time!

¹⁴ For if I pray in a tongue, my spirit prays, but my mind is unfruitful. ¹⁵ So what shall I do? I will pray with my spirit, but I will also pray with my understanding; I will sing with my spirit, but I will also sing with my understanding.

These verses infer that when the New Testament talks about praying in the Spirit, it means praying in tongues. It is important to pray with your understanding (in English), but also to pray in tongues. Paul introduces something new which is also of great benefit: singing in the Spirit. I wish this was encouraged more. It is beautiful to hear a new song in angelic languages, and great to sing in tongues throughout the day (congregational singing in the Spirit seems to be exempt from the general prohibition on speaking out in tongues unless it is interpreted). Tongues serves as the oil that gets the Spirit flowing in your life.

Tongues primarily for private use

⁶ Now, brothers and sisters, if I come to you and speak in tongues, what good will I be to you, unless I bring you some revelation or knowledge or prophecy or word of instruction? ⁷ Even in the case of lifeless things that make sounds, such as the pipe or harp, how will anyone know what tune is being played unless there is a distinction in the notes? ⁸ Again, if the trumpet does not sound a clear call, who will get ready for battle? ⁹ So it is with you. Unless you speak intelligible words with your tongue, how will anyone know what you are saying? You will just be speaking into the air. ¹⁰ Undoubtedly there are all sorts of languages in the world, yet none of them is without meaning. ¹¹ If then I do not grasp the meaning of what someone is saying, I am a foreigner to the speaker, and the speaker is a foreigner to me. ¹² So it is with you.

Since you are eager for gifts of the Spirit, try to excel in those that build up the church.
16 Otherwise when you are praising God in the Spirit, how can someone else, who is now put in the position of an inquirer, say "Amen" to your thanksgiving, since they do not know what you are saying? 17 You are giving thanks well enough, but no one else is edified.

19 But in the church I would rather speak five intelligible words to instruct others than ten thousand words in a tongue.

Paul spends significant time emphasizing the superiority of prophecy, because it edifies the whole church. But he has just described the benefits of tongues, so he certainly is not putting it down. Somehow the Corinthians had gotten into excessive tongues speaking during services, instead of focusing on what would edify the whole church.

20 Brothers and sisters, stop thinking like children. In regard to evil be infants, but in your thinking be adults. 21 In the Law it is written:
"With other tongues
  and through the lips of foreigners
I will speak to this people,
  but even then they will not listen to me,
says the Lord."

To finish this thought, Paul quotes Isaiah, to say that even the gift of tongues would not touch a hardened heart. It is a sign of immaturity to be overly focused on tongues ("*stop thinking like children*").

Guidance on the use of tongues

I thank God that I speak in tongues more than all of you (18).

If you have the gift of tongues (an angelic prayer language), use it! I have talked with elderly saints who proudly say: "Praise God! Thirty years ago the Lord baptized me in the Spirit and I spoke in tongues." But they never spoke in tongues since! They never developed the gift. It is easy to forget tongues' primary purpose (helping you pray and edifying yourself) when the focus is on tongues as a sign.

Nobody will care if you walk down the street praying (quietly) in tongues. I do it a lot. They will just think you are from another country, or talking on your cel phone! If I go several days without speaking in tongues, I have to check what is going on in my spirit, because I have found that there is a direct relationship to my spiritual health. When I am walking in the Spirit I pray in tongues a lot.

If God has given you this gift, you can start speaking in tongues whenever you want to. You don't have to wait for some special feeling or an anointed service. If you are just starting out, you may find yourself repeating the same word and wonder if you are just making it up. Like a baby learning to talk, you start simply, but with practice your tongues become more fluent. Sadly, many never bother developing it.

So if the whole church comes together and everyone speaks in tongues, and inquirers or unbelievers come in, will they not say that you are out of your mind? (23)

A service where everyone is yelling out in tongues doesn't impress anyone, especially not God. It can be a stumbling block to those who aren't used to tongues, and confirms unbelievers' suspicion that Christians (especially of the Pentecostal/Charismatic bent) are crazy. In church, pray or worship in tongues so no one else hears it.

For this reason the one who speaks in a tongue should pray that they may interpret what they say (13).

If anyone speaks in a tongue, two—or at the most three—should speak, one at a time, and someone must interpret. If there is no interpreter, the speaker should keep quiet in the church and speak to himself and to God (27-28).

There is a difference between public interpreted tongues (which function like prophecy), and the private prayer language. If someone is in the habit of speaking out in tongues without interpretation, a leader should talk to them. Unfortunately, there are people who like to call attention to themselves and discredit the genuine gift. If a message is given in tongues, pray for interpretation, and wait for God to give it. It is helpful to explain to the church what is going on, for those not accustomed to tongues.

Therefore, my brothers and sisters, be eager to prophesy, and do not forbid speaking in tongues (39).

Churches that forbid tongues are in sin. Good, biblical, teaching on tongues is rare, but much needed.

"I would like every one of you to speak in tongues." (Paul)

161

Receiving the gift of tongues

Would you like an angelic language to help you pray and build yourself up at any time? I see nothing in Scripture to indicate that God wouldn't want you to have that gift. I have known people who feel second class because they begged for tongues and never received it. I don't understand that, but we have to trust in God's sovereignty. If you are open and have asked but never received it, praise God. I guess he feels you are doing just fine in English. We never want to create division between haves and have nots, and we never want to make up tongues just to please others.

I received the gift as a young Christian in college. One day I was alone, reading Merlin Carother's book *Power in Praise*. With my heart full of praise I started worshiping the Lord and suddenly, without even realizing it, I found myself worshiping in tongues. It was like a dam had burst in my heart and the words just poured out like rivers of living water.

How can you receive this gift?

Since it is a gift, simply ask God for it, with an open heart. Tell him you desire more intimate communication. Give your tongue to the Lord. Some find it hard to let go of the feeling that it is weird, or they don't need it, or don't want to be fanatical. If that is you, confess it to the Lord. Those who look down on "tongues-speakers" and insist they will never speak in tongues are probably the ones who truly need it as a point of surrender to the Lord.

- Search your heart and confess any sin. Sin will quench the flow of the Spirit.

- Give your life to Christ again and ask him to fill you with his Spirit.

- Start praying, giving thanks, or praising him. Come into his presence, and don't rush it. Often you will feel something filling your heart, rising up in your throat, and filling your mouth. Open your mouth and just say whatever comes out.

- Sometimes it is good to start with sighs or *"groans too deep for words"* (Romans 8:26), allowing yourself to deeply breathe in the Spirit, and breathe out whatever words he may give you.

- You may want to ask someone who speaks in tongues or believes in it to lay hands on you and pray for you.

If you have already spoken in tongues but for some reason no longer use it, I pray this would be a spark the Spirit would use to stir up the gift. If you were taught that tongues are not for today, I believe the Holy Spirit will touch your heart as you reflect on Scripture and give you a desire for a prayer language. If you have been asking God for help in your prayer life, this is it! *I would like every one of you to speak in tongues.*

23

God's Order for His Church

1 Corinthians 14:26-40

This chapter is full of controversy! We have talked about tongues and prophecy, and still have to look at God's plan for order in church services. That seems innocent enough, but then Paul talks about the role of women in church, and we once again have to decide if we will accept what God's Word says – even if it is not popular today.

How to conduct worship services

26 What then shall we say, brothers and sisters? When you come together, each of you has a hymn, or a word of instruction, a revelation, a tongue or an interpretation. Everything must be done so that the church may be built up. 27 If anyone speaks in a tongue, two—or at the most three—should speak, one at a time, and someone must interpret.28 If there is no interpreter, the speaker should keep quiet in the church and speak to himself and to God.

29 Two or three prophets should speak, and the others should weigh carefully what is said. 30 And if a revelation comes to someone who is sitting down, the first speaker should stop. 31 For you can all prophesy in turn so that everyone may be instructed and encouraged. [32] The spirits of prophets are subject to the control of prophets. [33] For God is not a God of disorder but of peace—as in all the congregations of the Lord's people.

That is a far cry from what we see in most church services today! I recently heard someone asking what time the "show" was at a huge church near us. It seems like church is more of a performance, with a slick worship band and great preacher to entertain, charge us up, and make us feel good. Sort of like a game at a stadium. The question is, do you want to be in the game, or sit and watch?

Scripture portrays church as a body, with every member having an important part to play when we meet together. You come to church full, ready to share and encourage others, instead of arriving empty, expecting to be filled by the music, preaching, and (hopefully) the anointing. Obviously, it is hard for everyone to participate in a church with thousands of members. Small groups become essential, where community can be experienced and spiritual gifts exercised. It is beautiful to have a service where everyone is united in the Spirit, waiting on the Lord, with the Spirit guiding one to start in prayer, another to lead out with a song of worship, another to read a Scripture, another to bring a prophetic word - and all of it flowing together. It means that the pastor or leader has to give up control to the Holy Spirit. That is risky, because people will get out of the Spirit and into the flesh. Someone will want to sing their favorite song every week, another will use prayer as an opportunity to share some gossip, and another will bring a questionable Scripture interpretation. It is up to the pastor or leader to intervene at that point. But it is all part of learning to function as a body.

God is not limited to one type of worship. So-called "liturgical worship," which follows the same format every week and usually has a printed order of service, can be powerfully used by the Lord. Actually, churches that pride themselves on giving the Spirit freedom - and not having a printed order of service - usually follow the same pattern week after week. With the emphasis on great sounding worship bands, almost all music is planned ahead. God forbid they don't look professional on TV or the internet! It's not wrong to plan a service, but it is great to let the Spirit lead which songs to sing.

Freedom doesn't mean disorder. If the Spirit is present, there will be order and peace. The goal is to give the Spirit freedom as leaders are sensitive to him. They need to teach and model the church functioning as a body, and encourage various gifts to be expressed in the worship. A true worship service that pleases God requires the Spirit's presence and anointing. My guess is we rely more on the musical ability of the band and the preacher's rhetorical skills. We know what people want and we give it to them, and they are happy if they leave feeling good. We don't even need the Spirit, or give him the chance to really have his way. The test for each part of a service is: Does it edify? Does it build up the body? I think we waste a lot of time, and interrupt the flow of the Spirit, with announcements, the offering, and other fillers that don't really edify.

Women's participation in the worship service

[33] As in all the congregations of the Lord's people, [34] women should remain silent in the churches. They are not allowed to speak, but must be in submission, as the law says. [35] If they want to inquire about something, they should ask their own husbands at home; for it is disgraceful for a woman to speak in

the church.

36 Or did the word of God originate with you? Or are you the only people it has reached? 37 If anyone thinks they are a prophet or otherwise gifted by the Spirit, let them acknowledge that what I am writing to you is the Lord's command. 38 But if anyone ignores this, they will themselves be ignored.

To twenty-first century ears this sounds hopelessly chauvinistic and outdated. How far do we really have to go in following everything the Bible says? And how do you interpret this in light of other Scripture?

The study of women in the church is a long and difficult one. Among the many books on the topic, the best I have found is *Women and Ministry* by Dan Doriani. I can't possibly cover all the angles here, but it really troubles me how much manipulation takes place to get around passages we don't like. It is not up to us to cut out parts of the Bible. Don't become a judge of God's Word.

This word is not only for a particular situation in Corinth. Paul says it is the practice in all the churches. There are times when Paul states that something is his opinion, and not God's command. But here he says it is the Lord's command, and he has strong words for someone who chooses to ignore it.

It is clear that women can speak in some situations. In the same letter (11:5) Paul speaks of women praying and prophesying. Acts 21:9 mentions Phillip's four unmarried daughters who prophesied. Spiritual gifts are given without regard to gender (Joel 2:28-29), although it appears the five ministry offices are restricted to men. Here I believe Paul has in mind the same message he shared in 1 Timothy 2:11-14: *A woman should learn in quietness and full submission. I do not permit a woman to teach or to assume authority over a man; she must be quiet. For Adam was formed first, then Eve. And Adam was not the one deceived; it was the woman who was deceived and became a sinner.* This is not a cultural issue, but is based on creation, and submission, as it is taught in many other passages. It is very difficult to honor the word and still argue that women should be pastors or exercise authority over men.

⁴⁰*But everything should be done in a fitting and orderly way.*

God has established order and determined how things are to work in his creation, society, the church, the family, and the individual. The world today is in rebellion to authority, and that rebellion has infected the church. When we fail to do things in a fitting way, according to the order God has established, we all suffer. In this chapter Paul has laid out clear guidelines for order in the church. We may not like them or agree with them, but our job is to submit to the Word and put it into practice. May God help us order our churches according to his plan. That is when we will see his blessing.

24

The Messenger, the Message, and the Recipients

1 Corinthians 15:1-11

¹¹Whether, then, it is I or they, this is what we preach, and this is what you believed. (11)

Three essential elements of ministry are present in this one verse: A messenger, a message, and an audience that receives that message.

The messenger

⁷ Then he appeared to James, then to all the apostles, ⁸ and last of all he appeared to me also, as to one abnormally born. ⁹ For I am the least of the apostles and do not even deserve to be called an apostle, because I persecuted the church of God. ¹⁰ But by the grace of God I am what I am, and his grace to me was not without effect. No, I worked harder than all of them—yet not I, but the grace of God that was with me.

Jesus appeared! He's alive! God took the initiative and came to us in Jesus Christ, revealing God's nature. Have you had an encounter with the living Christ? You need to if you are going to share a living message. God is still calling messengers. He is not looking for volunteers. Paul felt he was the least of the apostles, but if God calls you, he will use you despite your past. Paul wasn't one of the Twelve. He was "*abnormally born*" - a word that can apply to a stillbirth or aborted fetus. The Amplified Bible says "*no better than an unperfected fetus among living men.*" Talk about feeling small or less than others! He was ashamed of his past. He would never forget Stephen's face as the stones killed him. Paul had approved of the stoning! He had been Christ's enemy, persecuting the church. Everything about him seemed wrong, and his critics were quick to point that out! But he refused to allow Satan to condemn him or stop him from being obedient to his calling. God loves using people like Paul! He loves to honor the ones despised by the world. Have you felt you don't qualify to be a messenger? You may feel different. You don't fit in. You wonder how God could use someone who has messed up like you have. Don't underestimate what God can do.

Paul was last and least. He didn't deserve the title of apostle, but God uses the weak. The last will be first. You may feel unworthy. You may not have others' education, success, speaking ability, good family, or good looks. It doesn't matter. It just confirms that it is not about you, but about God and his power. It is only by God's grace that you are what you are. Don't deceive yourself into thinking it was your hard work, charm, or talents. If God has given you a successful ministry, he deserves all the glory. You don't have to earn God's favor for him to bless you or use you; it is pure grace. Three times Paul mentions grace in these verses! You can't make it as a messenger on your own, without grace! We need to live all of life trusting in God's unmerited favor. God's grace was not "without effect," or (a better translation) fruitless. When God's grace is at work in your life, there will be fruit. If there has been no effect on your life, no fruit produced, examine yourself to see if you may be relying on your own efforts.

It sounds confusing: once we give up our own efforts and rely on God's grace, he motivates us to work harder! Ministry is hard work. I thank God for the many who work tirelessly for the Gospel, but some are simply lazy. Work with all your heart through the grace God gives you, for his glory.

The message

³ For what I received I passed on to you as of first importance: that Christ died for our sins according to the Scriptures, ⁴ that he was buried, that he was raised on the third day according to the Scriptures, ⁵ and that he appeared to Cephas, and then to the Twelve. ⁶ After that, he appeared to more than five hundred of the brothers and sisters at the same time, most of whom are still living, though some have fallen asleep.

God also gave us the message; we just pass on what we have received. It is not up to us to think up something new to attract more people. Don't add to the Word of God. Our faith is based on its authority. The message is very simple: Jesus Christ. We are sinners separated from God. We can't save ourselves. Only a perfect sacrifice could satisfy God's righteousness and keep us from eternal death. Jesus died on the cross for your sins, as prophesied in the Old Testament, was buried, and rose on the third day. Jesus is alive! Hundreds of people, many of whom were still living at the time Paul wrote, were witnesses of his resurrection. There is no doubt that Jesus rose. He conquered sin, death, and Satan. His victory now becomes our victory. That resurrection is the theme of this chapter.

Is this message the foundation of your preaching? Or do you feel like Jesus is not exciting enough; that you must preach what itching ears want to hear? Do you avoid uncomfortable issues like sin and the cost of discipleship? Of course we offer the "meat" of the Word to the church as well, but this message is of first importance.

The recipients

¹Now, brothers and sisters, I want to remind you of the gospel I preached to you, which you received and on which you have taken your stand. ²By this gospel you are saved, if you hold firmly to the word I preached to you. Otherwise, you have believed in vain.

You can have a great messenger and powerful message, but if there is no one to receive it (if you are preaching to an empty church), it doesn't do much good. God equips and prepares us for a purpose. The harvest (the recipients) is plentiful but the workers are few. God is preparing people to hear this message right now. The job of those who hear is to receive it, by faith, believing it is true and applies to their lives. But it is not enough to just receive it. We must firmly hold to it and obey it. Doubts and trials will come, but Jesus is the rock, and we must hold him fast.

The Corinthians were experiencing the power of the Holy Spirit and his gifts, but in the busyness and excitement of church and its programs, they (like us) could easily forget about Jesus. The messenger must remind the people of this message, the heart of the Gospel.

There is a condition to our salvation: firmly holding to this message and putting it into practice. Persevering. Holding on and hanging in there. I know it is popular to believe that simply receiving the message by saying a little prayer guarantees your entry to heaven. It sounds good to those who aren't willing to repent and forsake their sin, but it is not biblical. We embrace the message when we first accept Christ, but we must continue to embrace it - and him! If we reject the message and deny Christ's lordship in our lives we are failing to meet a basic condition of our salvation. It is possible to believe in vain (AMP: *All for nothing*)! If you fail to persevere and hold on to Jesus and his Word, your faith is in vain. In fact, I would say it is worse - even dangerous - to have a false confidence that all is well because you said a prayer years ago, even if you are not walking with Jesus today.

Jesus gives examples of believing in vain

Jesus' parable of the Sower presents the possibility of believing in vain:

"The farmer sows the word. Some people are like seed along the path, where the word is sown. As soon as they hear it, Satan comes and takes away the word that was sown in them. Others, like seed sown on rocky places, hear the word and at once receive it with joy. But since they have no root, they last only a short time. When trouble or persecution comes because of the word, they quickly fall away. Still others, like seed sown among thorns, hear the word; but the worries of this life, the deceitfulness of wealth and the desires for other things come in and choke the word, making it unfruitful. Others, like seed sown on good soil, hear the word, accept it, and produce a crop—some thirty, some sixty, some a hundred

times what was sown" (Mark 4:14-20).

The message and the messenger don't change. Each is faithful to their calling and purpose. The seed is top quality: God's Word, the Gospel. The only difference is the soil, the one receiving the message. Satan takes advantage of hard hearts to immediately snatch the seed sown in some people. Others have no root; they neither hold onto the Word nor put it into practice. When trouble or persecution comes because of their faith they fall away. They believed in vain. The same with the third group, which stayed in the Word and was active in church. Unfortunately, life's worries, greed, and the deceitfulness of money choke out the Word and they never produce fruit. They probably don't realize it, but they believed in vain. Only a quarter of the seed is sown in good soil, in those who hear the message, receive it, and produce a good crop. They stand firm and hold onto the Word.

Another example is found in Matthew 7:26-27:

"But everyone who hears these words of mine and does not put them into practice is like a foolish man who built his house on sand. The rain came down, the streams rose, and the winds blew and beat against that house, and it fell with a great crash."

The wise man built his house on an unshakable foundation, obedience to God's Word. This man heard the same Word and also built his house, but never bothered to put Jesus' words into practice. His house came crashing down when storms came against it. He had believed in vain.

Which one are you? Have you received this message? If you want to be saved, you can agree that this message is true and ask Jesus to take hold of your life right now. He wants to forgive your sins and give you a new life. It doesn't matter what you have done.

If you have already received the message, are you holding on? Holding fast to Jesus? Are troubles threatening to choke out the word? Is there a possibility that the deceitfulness of wealth and ungodly desires could result in you believing in vain? Are you in the middle of a storm right now? Have you put God's Word into practice? Or are you still trying to build a house on the sand?

Are you doing your part to sow the seed? If God has called you to share this message, he will give you the grace to work with all your heart for his glory.

25

The Importance of
Christ's Resurrection
1 Corinthians 15:12-34

You may not have been born yet, but back in the seventies there was a popular cross-over gospel singer named Andraé Crouch. One of his songs said:

But if heaven never was promised to me,
Neither God's promise to live eternally.
It's been worth just having the Lord in my life.

It sounds great, but Paul might have disagreed. In this passage he says: *If only for this life we have hope in Christ, we are of all people most to be pitied (most miserable)* (19). That is how critical the resurrection is to our faith. Many of us are so comfortable on earth that the promise of heaven seems distant - and maybe not even too attractive. I have heard many Christians question whether being in a non-stop worship service is really the way they want to spend eternity. The hope of heaven or threat of hell is not enough motivation for many to become Christians, and there is considerable doubt that there is life beyond the grave. That was true in Paul's day as well.

The resurrection of Christ is the cornerstone of our faith

¹² But if it is preached that Christ has been raised from the dead, how can some of you say that there is no resurrection of the dead? ¹³ If there is no resurrection of the dead, then not even Christ has been raised. ¹⁴ And if Christ has not been raised, our preaching is useless and so is your faith. ¹⁵ More than that, we are then found to be false witnesses about God, for we have testified about God that he raised Christ from the dead. But he did not raise him if in fact the dead are not raised. ¹⁶ For if the dead are not raised, then Christ has not been raised either. ¹⁷ And if Christ has not been raised, your faith is futile; you are still in your sins. ¹⁸ Then those also who have fallen asleep in Christ are lost.

If Christ did not rise:
- Our preaching is useless (in vain).
- Our faith is useless (in vain, empty, imaginary) and futile (mere delusion, fruitless).
- We are false witnesses (liars) about God.
- The dead are not raised.
- We are still in our sins (under the control and penalty of sin).
- The dead in Christ are lost.

Jesus led an exemplary life, and his sacrifice on the cross was an amazing demonstration of selfless love, but it really doesn't mean much without the hope and victory of the resurrection. If you are not convinced he rose, a great, short, book to read is Lee Stroebel's *The Case for Easter*.

The resurrection reveals God's plan for eternity

20 But Christ has indeed been raised from the dead, the firstfruits of those who have fallen asleep. 21 For since death came through a man, the resurrection of the dead comes also through a man. 22 For as in Adam all die, so in Christ all will be made alive. 23 But each in turn: Christ, the firstfruits; then, when he comes, those who belong to him. 24 Then the end will come, when he hands over the kingdom to God the Father after he has destroyed all dominion, authority and power. 25 For he must reign until he has put all his enemies under his feet. 26 The last enemy to be destroyed is death.27 For he "has put everything under his feet." Now when it says that "everything" has been put under him, it is clear that this does not include God himself, who put everything under Christ. 28 When he has done this, then the Son himself will be made subject to him who put everything under him, so that God may be all in all.

Here is a glimpse of the amazing future God has prepared for you:

1. Christ is the first fruits, the guarantee that you too will rise from the dead. There is a beautiful order in what God does. Christ is the second Adam. Just as Adam brought eternal death to our race, now Jesus brings eternal life to those who are *in* him, who *belong* to him.

2. Right now we are in a battle. Jesus reigns, but he still has many enemies. He is in the process of bringing everything under his feet. He already has that authority, given him by his Father, but many of his enemies are putting up a stiff fight. He is counting on his disciples (us) to help in that battle, and also share in the victory. He

will destroy all dominion, authority, and power in this world. Neither the USA nor any other great power will last forever. When the battle is over, the end will come. It may be possible to speed the process along by extending his kingdom and battling his enemies.

3. The Father has already given Jesus all dominion and power, even over Satan. He wants to share that dominion with us, so we can reign in this life.

4. Death is a serious enemy, the last enemy, an enemy that Christ defeated on the cross. Right now death still has dominion over us, but the resurrection of Christ is our guarantee that death has no hold on us. By faith we believe that Christ's victory over death is ours as well. God hates death even more than we do. There is no need to fear it.

5. God the Father has put everything under Christ's feet, but he himself will never be put under Christ. When Jesus has finished his task he will joyfully and proudly hand the kingdom over to his Father.

6. We shouldn't resist or fear submission. It is an important part of God's order. Christ willingly submits himself to his Father when he has completed everything. There is freedom and blessing in a healthy submission.

The final goal is that God would be all in all, supreme in every place in every way. The Amplified Bible says: *Everything to everyone, supreme, the indwelling, controlling factor of life,* and the New Living Translation: *Utterly supreme over everything everywhere.* Everything will come together in him (see Ephesians 1:9-10 and Romans 11:36). With death conquered, the separation between heaven and earth will be healed.

What the resurrection means for our daily lives

Now if there is no resurrection, what will those do who are baptized for the dead? If the dead are not raised at all, why are people baptized for them? (29)

This is a hard verse which we really don't understand. Mormons use it to justify baptism for the dead. The most common explanation is that relatives may have been baptized for some who died before getting baptized, but we can't build a doctrine or practice from one verse.

And as for us, why do we endanger ourselves every hour? I face death every day —yes, just as surely as I boast about you in Christ Jesus our Lord (30-31).

Paul was no stranger to near-death experiences, yet he was able to say *"to live is Christ and to die is gain"* because of his firm confidence in the resurrection. Without that, we would try to safeguard our lives at all costs. There would be no reason to put ourselves at risk.

If I fought wild beasts in Ephesus with no more than human hopes, what have I gained? If the dead are not raised, "Let us eat and drink, for tomorrow we die." (32)

This philosophy guides much of our world: Live life to the full today, with no worry about the consequences, because we don't know what tomorrow holds, and are uncertain about life after death. There is no motivation for holy living, so we would be foolish not to live it up now!

Do not be misled: "Bad company corrupts good character." (33)

We all know how easy it is to be corrupted by ungodly friends. We may think we can influence them for Christ, but too often it is the other way around. It doesn't mean we completely separate from the world, but we exercise real caution in how we relate to unsaved friends.

Come back to your senses as you ought, and stop sinning; for there are some who are ignorant of God —I say this to your shame (34).

Based on their lifestyle, Paul has real doubts about their salvation. Those who truly know God should be motivated to stop sinning. An adequate understanding of the resurrection is a strong incentive for holiness.

What about you?
- Are you really saved?
- Do you believe the living Christ is battling his enemies right now? Are you in that battle?
- Do you long for the day when everything will finally be under his feet and he will come and reign forever?
- Are you doing your part to hasten his coming, proclaiming his kingdom and taking authority over his enemies in his name?
- How is your walk? Are you walking in holiness? In the light of the resurrection?

26

Your Resurrection Body
1 Corinthians 15:35-58

Having proven there is a resurrection because we know that Christ rose from the dead, Paul now addresses the nature of our resurrected bodies.

- Jews believed the resurrected body would be the same body we have now.
- Greeks didn't believe in a resurrection.
- The Corinthian Christians were so "in the Spirit" that some believed they already had their immortal bodies!

What does the Bible say?

35 But someone will ask, "How are the dead raised? With what kind of body will they come?" 36 How foolish! What you sow does not come to life unless it dies. 37 When you sow, you do not plant the body that will be, but just a seed, perhaps of wheat or of something else. 38 But God gives it a body as he has determined, and to each kind of seed he gives its own body. 39 Not all flesh is the same: People have one kind of flesh, animals have another, birds another and fish another. 40 There are also heavenly bodies and there are earthly bodies; but the splendor of the heavenly bodies is one kind, and the splendor of the earthly bodies is another. 41 The sun has one kind of splendor, the moon another and the stars another; and star differs from star in splendor.

The resurrection body

Are you anxious to know what your new body will look like? Our mortal bodies give us an idea, but just as most plants bear little resemblance to the seeds they come from, so this body is like a seed that may give birth to something very different in eternity. We will be recognizable, but the glory of our resurrected bodies is probably beyond what we can imagine.

[42] *So will it be with the resurrection of the dead. The body that is sown is perishable, it is raised imperishable;* [43] *it is sown in dishonor, it is raised in glory; it is sown in weakness, it is raised in power;* [44] *it is sown a natural body, it is raised a spiritual body. If there is a natural body, there is also a spiritual body.*

Our bodies are:
- Perishable.
- Sown in dishonor.
- Sown in weakness.
- A natural body.

The resurrected body is:
- Raised imperishable.
- Raised in glory.
- Raised in power.
- A spiritual body.

We all have something about our bodies we would like to change. Can you imagine a perfect body, free of the limitations, pain, and sickness of this mortal body?

[45] *So it is written: "The first man Adam became a living being"; the*

last Adam, a life-giving spirit. ⁴⁶ The spiritual did not come first, but the natural, and after that the spiritual. ⁴⁷ The first man was of the dust of the earth; the second man is of heaven. ⁴⁸ As was the earthly man, so are those who are of the earth; and as is the heavenly man, so also are those who are of heaven. ⁴⁹ And just as we have borne the image of the earthly man, so shall we bear the image of the heavenly man. ⁵⁰ I declare to you, brothers and sisters, that flesh and blood cannot inherit the kingdom of God, nor does the perishable inherit the imperishable.

The first man (Adam):

- Became a living being.
- Was of the dust of the earth.
- We are like him.
- We have borne his image.
- Cannot inherit the kingdom of God.
- Cannot inherit the imperishable

The second man (Christ), and those who are in him:

- Is a life-giving spirit.
- Is of heaven.
- We become like the heavenly man.
- We bear the image of the heavenly man.
- We inherit the kingdom
- We inherit the imperishable

Here on earth we have the natural body that came down from Adam. The new body will be very different, bearing a heavenly image, the image of Christ.

A mystery revealed

[51] Listen, I tell you a mystery: We will not all sleep, but we will all be changed — [52] in a flash, in the twinkling of an eye, at the last trumpet. For the trumpet will sound, the dead will be raised imperishable, and we will be changed. [53] For the perishable must clothe itself with the imperishable, and the mortal with immortality. [54] When the perishable has been clothed with the imperishable, and the mortal with immortality, then the saying that is written will come true: "Death has been swallowed up in victory."

A biblical mystery is not a whodunit, but rather something we can't discern in the natural, something hidden which God chooses to reveal. This is one of several mysteries in the Bible:

- Though most people will die, some will be alive when Jesus returns.
- We will all be changed (receive a new body, the perishable clothed with the imperishable, the mortal with immortality).
- The transformation will be instantaneous – in a flash, the twinkling of an eye.
- It will happen at the sound of the last trumpet (see Matthew 24:31 and Revelation 11:15).
- At that moment, the dead will rise with a new, incorruptible, body.

This is the final victory over death, the end of death.

[55] "Where, O death, is your victory? Where, O death, is your sting?"

56 The sting of death is sin, and the power of sin is the law.

As you grieve over a dying loved one it seems that death's victory and sting is very real. It surely hurts, but we keep our eyes on eternity, the victory Jesus won on the cross, and his resurrection. This isn't pie in the sky – it is real, and should fill our lives with hope and anticipation. It is a powerful word our world needs today, especially those facing death; not an empty assurance that they will be in heaven, but sharing the full story of Jesus and what he has done.

Sin brought death into our race, and is the sting of death we feel every day. But Jesus has set us free from sin, and the more we overcome sin the weaker the sting of death will be. The power of sin was the law – but we are no longer under the law. We are under grace, filled with God's Spirit, and walking in relationship with Jesus. When we fall back into legalism, sin becomes more of a problem, especially when we try to be "good Christians" in our own strength.

Your labor in the Lord is not in vain

57 But thanks be to God! He gives us the victory through our Lord Jesus Christ. 58 Therefore, my dear brothers and sisters, stand firm. Let nothing move you. Always give yourselves fully to the work of the Lord, because you know that your labor in the Lord is not in vain.

The resurrection isn't just good theology. Both the certainty of Christ's resurrection and the hope of our own resurrection should have an impact on our daily lives. God gives us the victory through Jesus. We are still in a serious battle with sin, death and Satan, but victory is ours. Are you walking in that victory? It is a gift, only available through a relationship with Jesus Christ. You may have friends and family who don't know Jesus and are destined for defeat. Tell them about the victory that is available to them!

Stand firm. Let nothing move you. False doctrines, temptations, and discouragement will come and try to make you unstable and confused, like the waves on the ocean. Stand firm on the basic truths taught in Scripture, and especially on Jesus. Make sure your life is not built on sand, but on the rock, which Matthew 7:24 tells us involves putting Jesus' words into action. What storms are coming against you right now? What is threatening to move you away from Jesus? Stand firm! And stand with other believers who share your commitment. It is easy to move an individual, but much harder to move a group that is knit together!

Always give yourself to the Lord's work (NLT: *work enthusiastically*)! Spanish versions say "keep growing," or "progressing." The idea is ongoing development of your work, on a constant basis. The Lord's work is to be a part of our daily lives, and there should be steady growth in it. You probably shouldn't be doing the same thing you did five or ten years ago. If you are, maybe that is why you are losing interest in it!

How can we continue that work in the face of discouragement? Scripture promises that your labor in the Lord is not in vain (AMP: *never wasted, futile, or to no purpose*).

- The key words there may be *in the Lord.* Too many people are doing their own thing and calling it God's work. What you do in the flesh will not endure.
- Are you discouraged? If you are finding your work unfruitful, take a moment to examine yourself before the Lord to make sure he is the one directing it. If he is, his

word will not return to him void.

- Obediently do what he has called you to do and leave the results in his hands. Only eternity will reveal the full extent of what you have done.

Praise God! Jesus rose from the dead! You will rise to eternal life! God has a glorious future for us!

27

Giving with Integrity
1 Corinthians 16:1-4

A s you might expect for someone finishing a letter, Paul has some personal concerns. First is a collection for Jewish brothers in Jerusalem, where persecution has left them impoverished. The help of Gentile believers would have been impressive, since even Jews who believed in Jesus harbored some lingering prejudice. It is a great example of believers helping those of another race or culture, affirming the model in Acts of sharing wealth to bring some financial equality. Unfortunately, that is not the case today. Yes, American Christians, the richest in the history of the world, do give a lot. Yet they still maintain a lifestyle radically better than the majority of their brothers throughout the world. Most of us feel overwhelmed at the thought of doing something about it, but Paul's guidelines provide insights on how it could be done.

¹ Now about the collection for the Lord's people: Do what I told the Galatian churches to do. ² On the first day of every week, each one of you should set aside a sum of money in keeping with your income, saving it up, so that when I come no collections will have to be made. ³ Then, when I arrive, I will give letters of introduction to the men you approve and send them with your gift to Jerusalem. ⁴ If it seems advisable for me to go also, they will accompany me.

- A recognized authority outside the local church (such as an apostle or denominational leader) initiates an appeal for money, along with instructions on how to collect it.

- They need to be familiar with the needs among the churches and ensure integrity in the collections.

- Paul didn't pressure anyone to give, but his expectation was that *each one* would participate. He felt it would be best to set money aside each Sunday, possibly in a worship service. This enables each person to reflect, pray, and follow their own conscience, instead of being pressured to give a large amount when Paul comes. He wants to use his visit to build up the church and not waste time begging them to give more. I have actually been in services where visiting preachers spend more time on the offering than the preaching of the Word! It is the responsibility of each person or family to set aside and save their money, and give it to Paul when he comes.

- They should give in keeping with their income (AMP: *as he has prospered*). The poor usually give proportionately much more than the wealthy. If God has prospered you, it is your responsibility to share that blessing with others.

- They don't just send a check, but make it personal, with the church itself choosing representatives to take the money to Jerusalem, a pretty significant trip at that time! This would ensure that neither Paul (in this case), nor any organization, would take some of the money, and it builds a bridge between the two churches. Paul is still in charge - he will give letters of introduction and, if possible, go with them.

Dealing with money can invite abuses and bring out the worst in people. Robbing a fellow Christian is serious. Be careful with your money; give only to someone you trust, and have safeguards in place to ensure integrity. Every church has the responsibility to openly report how much money they receive and how they spend it, and everyone who gives to a church has the right to know where their money is going.

What a privilege to help fellow believers! May God prosper you and give you wisdom in how to use that money!

28

Your Future is in God's Hands
1 Corinthians 16:5-12

Paul spoke with great conviction about Christian doctrine and practice, but his personal life was full of difficulty and uncertainly. How does he plan and approach the future under those circumstances? The only thing he can say for sure is he will visit them:

5 After I go through Macedonia, I will come to you —for I will be going through Macedonia.

He is anxious to spend time with them, but was willing to wait to make certain that time would be meaningful. He also hoped they would help him as he continued on his journey, but look at how he says it:

*6 **Perhaps** I will stay with you for a while, or even spend the winter, so that you can help me on my journey, **wherever I go**. 7 For I do not want to see you now and make only a passing visit; I **hope** to spend some time with you, **if the Lord permits**.*

There is nothing wrong with having hopes and desires, or making tentative plans. Paul was obviously thinking about the future, but he wouldn't make a firm agenda months in advance. He had learned that the Lord may not permit us to carry out what seem like good plans. Our danger is getting so locked into our own agenda that we don't leave room for God to guide us. And then, out of pride, we refuse to back out because it would make us look bad, even if we sense God saying something different. Two Scriptures come to mind that describe Paul, and should describe us as well:

> *"The wind blows wherever it pleases. You hear its sound, but you cannot tell where it comes from or where it is going. So it is with everyone born of the Spirit"* (John 3:8).

Spirit-led people may look like they don't know what they are doing. Their lives probably will not make a lot of sense to those immersed in the world system.

> *Now listen, you who say, "Today or tomorrow we will go to this or that city, spend a year there, carry on business and make money." Why, you do not even know what will happen tomorrow. What is your life? You are a mist that appears for a little while and then vanishes. Instead, you ought to say, "If it is the Lord's will, we will live and do this or that"* (James 4:13-15).

An open door

Presently, an open door is telling Paul it is God's will to stay in Ephesus:

⁸But I will stay on at Ephesus until Pentecost, ⁹ because a great door for effective work has opened to me, and there are many who oppose me.

There seems to be a contradiction. He wants to stay there to take advantage of an impressive opportunity that has opened for effective ministry - yet at the same time there are many who oppose him. Some would take the opposition to mean it is time to leave, but opposition doesn't necessarily indicate a closed door for ministry; it can mean the opposite. Great opportunity will probably be accompanied by great opposition.

Paul sends Timothy

Since it will be awhile before he can visit them, Paul is sending his beloved "son," Timothy. But instead of being confident that this church he founded would receive him in Christian love, he fears the worst:

[10]*When Timothy comes, see to it that he has nothing to fear while he is with you, for he is carrying on the work of the Lord, just as I am.* [11]*No one, then, should treat him with contempt. Send him on his way in peace so that he may return to me. I am expecting him along with the brothers.*

Paul has several concerns for Timothy:
- He might have reason to be afraid. The New Living Translation says *Don't intimidate him.* Paul is concerned they might take advantage of his youth and inexperience to bully him!
- He might be treated with contempt (AMP: *despised, treated as if he were of no account, slighted*).
- He might not be viewed as a true Christian worker.

- He might not be sent on his way in peace.

Apollos refuses to go

Another strange situation involves Apollos, who was also close to Paul. Despite Paul's insistent urging, he stubbornly refused to visit them, choosing instead to go at a time that would be convenient for him:

¹²Now about our brother Apollos: I strongly urged him to go to you with the brothers. He was quite unwilling to go now, but he will go when he has the opportunity.

I like to think of Paul as being so in step with the Spirit that things flowed smoothly for him, with clear direction about what he was to do and where he was to go. We like control and predictability, but when you are serving Christ you probably won't have either. I think of Jesus' words in John 8:19-20:

> *Then a teacher of the law came to him and said, "Teacher, I will follow you wherever you go." Jesus replied, "Foxes have dens and birds have nests, but the Son of Man has no place to lay his head."*

We don't have control!

We hope that things go well for those we have discipled and encouraged in ministry, but Timothy faced prejudice, mistreatment, and rejection, from a church that Paul founded and supervised! And Apollos was openly rebellious to his wishes. Paul had no control over the Corinthians, Timothy, or Apollos. We want control in our churches and homes so that things go well and the Lord is honored. We feel it is our responsibility as husbands, fathers, and pastors to ensure that things are done right, but we don't have that control. We have influence, and Paul had great influence based on his integrity and prior experience with the Corinthians. But ultimately, we have to leave the results in the Lord's hands.

If you find yourself in a "fog", with things far less clear than you thought they would be, the Lord wants to encourage you. Maybe others have even implied that you are confused, or perhaps you are like Timothy and have been mistreated by the church. Don't let those experiences discourage you or keep you from being obedient to the Lord! Be careful of being an Apollos and fighting what mature men of God are encouraging you to do. Even though there may be many against you, keep ministering as long as the Lord gives you an open door!

29

A Real Man
1 Corinthians 16:13-24

This letter has been full of thought-provoking challenges, and now he closes with three that can transform your daily life.

1. Be a man

¹³ Be on your guard; stand firm in the faith; be courageous; be strong. ¹⁴ Do everything in love.

- The NIV "be courageous" is politically correct, but grammatically incorrect. The Greek says *be a man,* or *act like a man.* What a shame we are afraid to tell men to be men. We need true men more than ever! A real man is a godly man. Paul writes this because it is possible even for a Christian to abdicate his position and authority and *not* be a man. My brother, act like a man! Be a man! Man up!

- Be on your guard, be alert. As men we are called to be on guard for our families, vigilant for any physical danger or spiritual attack.
    - o Be alert to the kinds of people and things your children are involved with.
    - o Be on your guard against temptations with other

women, pornography, and ungodly influences that come into your home.
- o Pastors are called to be shepherds, keeping the sheep safe from wolves that devour the flock.

- Stand firm in the faith.
  - o We have seen many things in this letter that could undermine our faith and walk in the Lord. The only way to survive with all the pressures around us is to stand firm on the Word of God and our faith in Jesus Christ.
  - o Men are called to be pillars of society. Traditionally we gave strength to our wives and children, but many men are weak and unsteady today, having nothing to stand on, even looking to their woman for strength. They have found what our culture presents as manly and valuable to be inadequate.

- Be strong.
  - o The ideal man is physically, emotionally, and spiritually strong. What man wants to be known as weak? Men spend significant time and money at the gym to at least look strong. Too bad we don't dedicate the same effort to being spiritually and emotionally strong. The fact is it is easier to lift weights than to get down on our knees.
  - o If you exercise your faith by putting it into practice you will find yourself getting stronger.
  - o Some think strong men fight and dominate women and don't cry. It is hard for us to confess

weakness to anyone, but part of true strength is acknowledging our weakness before God and allowing him to renew our strength as we wait on him.

- o You can't just command someone to be strong. The command here is to strengthen yourself, to grow in strength. God has given you the means to do that with a steady diet of the Word, prayer, and fellowship.

- Do everything in love. That is not the first characteristic many look for in a man, but it would make a tremendous difference with our children, wives, churches, and even our jobs. Make it your aim to be a man of love. Not wishy washy sentimental love, but the sacrificial love Christ demonstrated when he went to the cross. God is love, and a real man is a man of love.

2. A real man is a servant, knowing when to submit and how to exercise authority

[15] You know that the household of Stephanas were the first converts in Achaia, and they have devoted themselves to the service of the Lord's people. I urge you, brothers and sisters, [16] to submit to such people and to everyone who joins in the work and labors at it. [17] I was glad when Stephanas, Fortunatus and Achaicus arrived, because they have supplied what was lacking from you. [18] For they refreshed my spirit and yours also. Such men deserve recognition.

As Paul's co-workers did, devote yourself to serving the Lord's people. Be a servant, as Christ demonstrated and commanded us, instead of seeking position or using others. Look for those with servant's hearts to be over you in the Lord.

- Properly position yourself in the flow of God's authority, so you will have authority in your home, church, and sphere of influence.
  - o You gain that authority by submitting to those God places over you.
  - o Paul urges us to submit to *anyone* who labors for the Lord, but particularly those who *serve* the Lord's people. Part of submitting is joining them in their work.
  - o Ask God to give you discernment so you submit to those who are true servants and really working for the Lord - and not for themselves or someone else. Not everyone deserves your submission.
  - o Paul affirmed these men - you may need to ask an apostle or church leader to recommendation who you should submit to.

- Instead of draining others, ask God to enable you to supply what they need and refresh their spirits.
  - o How have others refreshed your spirit? How can you do the same?
  - o Paul says he was glad when these men arrived and ministered to him. People will be glad when you come around, because you will be known as someone who is refreshing!

- Give recognition to those who deserve it. This is tricky, because it can easily give rise to jealousy. Too often those who don't necessarily deserve the recognition get it, and those who truly deserve it get overlooked.
  - o Make it a point in your ministry to recognize

those who deserve it.

- o We sometimes shy away from that for fear of making them prideful, but ask the Lord to show you appropriate ways to recognize them.
- o Be sure to tell those who have ministered into your life that you appreciate it.
- o Don't be afraid to go overboard with affirmation and encouragement. Few people get too much. You don't do it to be popular, but it will establish good relationships with those over and under you.

3. A real man values relationships

[19] The churches in the province of Asia send you greetings. Aquila and Priscilla greet you warmly in the Lord, and so does the church that meets at their house. [20] All the brothers and sisters here send you greetings. Greet one another with a holy kiss.

[21] I, Paul, write this greeting in my own hand.

[22] If anyone does not love the Lord, let that person be cursed! Come, Lord!

[23] The grace of the Lord Jesus be with you.

[24] My love to all of you in Christ Jesus. Amen.

Men have a hard time maintaining relationships. Women have a lot to teach us here. But a real man has learned the value of relationships and gives them appropriate priority. It is too easy for young men to destroy relationships and find themselves alone as they reach middle age.

- Be warm – not cold. Priscilla and Aquila greet them *warmly*. They greet each other with a holy kiss (the sanctified version of a common greeting in that day). Paul's final words are an assurance of his love for all of them. Some of it is cultural, but be affectionate, be warm, in your own church and with Christians everywhere.

- Maintain regular communication with Christians worldwide. Paul wrote many letters. Hardly anyone writes letters anymore, but Skype, call, send Emails, texts, or whatever else you can think of to stay in touch. Establish communication with churches in other cultures and countries. Perhaps through a mission trip find some believers you can regularly correspond with – and be faithful in doing so. If you tell someone you are going to stay in touch with them, do it. You are part of a world-wide brotherhood – enjoy it!

- Open your home to be used for the Lord. The only real ministry couple in the New Testament jointly pastored a church which met in their home.

While maintaining that fellowship, we are mindful of three realties:

- Our love for Jesus is even more important than our love for others. Loving Jesus is such a critical part of being a Christian that Paul doesn't hesitate to say that anyone who doesn't love the Lord is cursed.

- Though we are separated from other believers in a less-than-perfect world, we live with the hope and expectation of a coming kingdom. The cry of our heart, as was common at that time, is *Marana tha*, the Aramaic saying which means "Come, O Lord."

- Good as fellowship is, we don't rely on others. We maintain our fellowship through a common experience of God's grace. More than just being *with* us, the Greek here refers to Jesus *pouring* his grace all over us. I long for that! And I pray that he would pour his grace all over your life!

So we end our study of I Corinthians with three profound challenges:

1. Be a man!

2. Develop proper relationships with those over you and under you in the Lord.

3. Maintain loving relationships within the Body of Christ.

About the author:

Loren VanGalder started ministry in 1977 on staff with Inter-Varsity Christian Fellowship in New York City. He served as a chaplain with the Federal Bureau of Prisons for twenty one years. He continues a ministry as a spiritual father through web sites in English and Spanish (ASpiritualFather.com, Un PadreEspiritual.com). You can read his blog on the website. He has written many books in English and Spanish, available on Amazon.com. Loren has been married since 1982 and has one grown son.